Annie Fields, James Lodge

A Week Away from Time

Annie Fields, James Lodge

A Week Away from Time

ISBN/EAN: 9783744665919

Printed in Europe, USA, Canada, Australia, Japan

Cover: Foto ©Thomas Meinert / pixelio.de

More available books at **www.hansebooks.com**

A WEEK

AWAY FROM TIME.

BOSTON:
ROBERTS BROTHERS.
1887.

Copyright, 1887,
BY ROBERTS BROTHERS.

All rights reserved.

University Press:
JOHN WILSON AND SON, CAMBRIDGE.

CONTENTS.

	PAGE
PRELUDE	1
PROLOGUE	3
FIRST DAY	31
EVENING OF FIRST DAY	45
THE ITALIAN LETTER	55
SECOND DAY	75
SECOND DAY (*continued*)	85
EVENING OF SECOND DAY	101
THE STORY OF THE NECKLACE	103
THIRD DAY	125
EVENING OF THIRD DAY	141
THE LAWYER'S STORY	156
FOURTH DAY	167
EVENING OF FOURTH DAY	181
THE PALACE OF THE CLOSED WINDOW	191
FIFTH DAY	241
IN WAR-TIME; OR, ONLY A WOMAN'S SHOE	251
EVENING OF FIFTH DAY	283
SIXTH DAY	291

	PAGE
EVENING OF SIXTH DAY	295
THE VOICE	295
SEVENTH DAY	311
EVENING OF SEVENTH DAY	325
HAPPINESS	331

PRELUDE.

*Not under Olive nor the Tuscan pine
Sat this enchanted circle, as of old
They sat who heard Boccaccio's story told;
Yet are these spirits of a kindred line,
Who in their own Fair Harbor dream, and tell
The matter of their dreaming, while the spell
Of Indian sunsets and sea-breakers bold
Braids the romance wherewith their voices twine.*

What mortal could be sick or sorry here!
MATTHEW ARNOLD.

And all we met was fair and good,
  And all was good that Time could bring,
  And all the secret of the Spring
Moved in the chambers of the blood.

. . . And in my breast
  Spring wakens too, and my regret
  Becomes an April violet,
And buds and blossoms like the rest.
TENNYSON.

Ver illud erat. — VIRGIL.

PROLOGUE.

FAIR HARBOR.

FAIR HARBOR is one of the few places now left in the world which most people know nothing about. You may count on your fingers the men and women who have ever heard of it; and if you have the usual number of fingers, your list will come to an end first.

You are lucky if your own name find a place among the few who, led by chance or by natural selection, have come upon this singularly pretty and attractive bit of the very tip end of the heel of Cape Cod.[1] *I*

---

[1] *Thoreau calls Cape Cod " the bared and bended arm of Massachusetts," and Buzzard's Bay " the shoulder." Then Fair Harbor should be about the elbow, or " crazy bone."*

say come upon *advisedly; for you may live all unsuspecting in its near neighborhood, and lo! one day you turn a corner, either from the sea or the shore, and you are there! You may drive from Falmouth to Wood's Holl forty times, and never dream that if you had taken a certain turn down a green lane to your left you would have come after a little to what would seem to you enchanted ground, — the tiny harbor lying still and peaceful between wooded banks and high pastures and headlands stretching with graceful curves into the beautiful bay beyond. Or you might sail forever across from Mattapoisett down Buzzard's Bay and never steer near enough to the opening which, once seen, would draw you to the fairy inlet where the voices of sirens singing to your soul would bid you stay and be at rest.*

The southwestern breezes come fresh and cool up from Florida, up from the Gulf

Stream, soft as a dove's wing, bringing healing and balm to nerves hurt and overwrought by the "whips of the east wind" and the exciting air of other parts of the New England coast, hinting of icebergs while the hot sun burns. The wonderful quality of the air differentiates this whole region, and gives it a positive character of its own. Its special grace is temperance; fierce heat and sharp cold are here alike unknown.

At the time our story opens, Fair Harbor had, as I have said, few acquaintances, and so, few lovers. These few, however, made up for their rarity by an intensity of affection which somehow always assumed a very personal form, and this little fragment of the world became to them a beloved stronghold, intrenched in which they pointed their guns at the rest of mankind, demanded their sympathy or their life, and were themselves ready to die in defence of their citadel.

Margaret Temple passed a good deal of her time in this defensive attitude towards the Philistines, who did not know or did not care for her "pays de prédilection." She was one of the rare people who really love Nature among the thousands of false worshippers who wrong her by lip service while their hearts are far from her. Hers was no fitful homage, rendered at one season and denied at another. She walked through the days and years, doing loving and reverent service at the shrine of her Alma Mater, and her lamp burned as constantly and brightly in storm as in sunshine. "It is poor love," she used to say, "which cannot bear a frown or a stern look from the object of its affection, and which depends upon smiles and soft words for its loyalty."

She had discovered Fair Harbor while staying in its neighborhood one summer, after having been in Europe for several years. Her husband, for whose health they remained abroad, had died there, and her only brother went to Algiers to meet her and bring her home. The brother and sister, although quite different, were very near to each other, and had a true and intimate sympathy, which consanguinity by no means always implies, but which when it does exist in this special relationship is apt to be of very beautiful and perfect quality. Margaret's husband had been much older than herself (she was very young when she married), and their union was rather that of father and daughter. He became a confirmed invalid soon after their marriage, and her whole time and care had been concentrated upon him. Her grief at his death was as genuine as was everything about her, and for some years she lived very quietly, and saw only her own people and intimate friends. But she was still young; she had absolute health and wonderful vitality, and a freshness of sympathy and interest in people and things which made her life full and rich, and of much meaning to herself and others.

She was a handsome creature, tall and beautifully made, with a firm, elastic step, and bounding, joyful movements, as if only to be alive were a delight. When she was a young girl she used to say that she never opened her eyes in the morning without thanking God for another day,—and when she thanked Him on her knees for her "creation, preservation, and all the blessings of this life," it was with a profound gladness that she had been born into the world. The fairies who presided at her birth knew very well what they were doing when they gave her this supremely fortunate nature; knew that it was better than genius or gold; something which neither moth nor rust could corrupt; which thieves might covet, but could not steal. Not the tenderest sympathy for the sorrows and sins of others, nor a true humility with regard to herself; not the untruth or unkindness, which, like all of us, she sometimes encountered, could kill out the cheerful, hopeful, buoyant heart of her; and she still thanked God for her creation, and blessed Him for every day that He made, and said, " Let us rejoice and be glad in it!" Besides this dower of Nature, she had pre-eminently a good temper, *as distinguished from goodnature, or good-humor;* and if you have read the Rev. James Freeman Clarke's sermon on " The Education of the Temper," you will know what I mean; and if you have not, you had better do so.

In the spring of 188– Margaret went to Fair Harbor to pass a few weeks alone. She wrote to her brother Ralph (who had been living in New York lately, and was a flourishing stockbroker), and tried to persuade him to take a spring vacation and join her; but he said things were very lively just then, and made merry allusions to bulls and bears, — the fauna of Wall Street, he called them, which must have a prior claim over the flora of the Cape, — and, in fine, he could not come. Margaret meant to go across the water in June for the summer months, and Ralph promised to be with her at Fair Harbor when she returned in the autumn. So Margaret went to Fair Harbor alone, and, truth to say, didn't mind it in the least. She knew most of the towns in Barnstable County by heart, and the farmers and retired sea-captains and their families who lived in them liked her as well as she liked them, and welcomed her to their houses as their honored guest and good friend. They hardly understood her enthusiasm for the places they had known all their lives, and felt towards her very much as the White Mountain stage-driver did to the New York *tourist. "O no! I don't mind stoppin' a bit while you stare around. I dare say if I was down to York I should want to go gawpin' about same as you do up here!" Or like the Roman lady who said to the enthusiastic American, raving over the beauties of the Campagna, "But what you artists and 'forestieri' find to admire in this gloomy, hateful, malarial old spot is what we Italians cannot understand. Come out to my villa to-morrow, and I will show you lovely gardens and fountains and terraces. There, indeed, it is beautiful!"*

However, the good people on the Cape admired Margaret so much that they began to suspect there must be advantages in their surroundings to which they had hitherto been blind.

It was blossoming-time for the apple-trees and lilacs; the beach-plum all along the roadsides made white patches like soft snow-falls, and here and there formed hedges which looked like banks of snow in the distance, and as one came near, it smelt sweet as honey, with branches all clusters of delicate flowers like hawthorn. The birds welcomed Margaret with new songs that sounded all the sweeter for being old ones, and told her they had learned them for her sake. Song-sparrows, blue-birds, yellow-throated warblers, greeted her as they flew from bough to bough; she heard the quivering note and plaintive cry of the plover, and every now and then a friendly family of quails would cross the road in front of her in a leisurely manner, enjoying the immunity of life which a few months would endanger.

 She was stopping at an old farm-house in the lane that led down to the Harbor, with Captain Nye and his wife, old friends of hers, to whom her coming was always a festival. They had lost their only daughter many years ago, and they fancied that Margaret looked like her. "She has our Annie's eyes, mother, she surely do," the old captain had said the first time they ever saw Margaret, his own eyes full of tears. "She favors Annie greatly, and brings her right back to me, though 't is many a long year since we laid her in the churchyard yonder," the mother answered. "She'd 'a' been just about Mis' Temple's age now. Dear! dear! But the Lord knows best." "And blessed be His name!" said the old man reverently.

So there was nothing possible to be done which the worthy couple did not do for Margaret's comfort and satisfaction. Captain Nye was joint-owner of an oyster-bed in a little fresh-water river which ran into the bay near by; and "even the most benighted Bostonian knows," said Margaret, "that there are no oysters like Cape oysters; and the beauty of them is, that, unlike ordinary bivalves, they need no R *in the month to make them eatable.* They are just the nicest oysters in the world all the year round," — a proposition which she stated so sturdily that no one ever thought of disputing it. As to sea trout, they were a drug in her market. "They swim to my door," she declared, "and implore me to eat them." Certainly they came to her often, from up the Bay, generally in baskets, smothered in moss and mayflowers, with cards attached, bearing, not the names of the fish, but of their captors, laying themselves and their spoils at her feet.

One evening she was walking slowly back to the house from the wharf, where she had just left her row-boat. She had been rowing about the little harbor in the sunset, exploring the pretty coves she had explored so often, or floating with oars at rest, feasting on the glory of color in sky and sea, dreaming dreams with half-shut eyes, till

Prologue. 15

the young May moon smiled at her over her right shoulder (she held a good deal to that), and one by one the stars shone.

As she walked up the lane to the farmhouse, a handsome red Irish setter came bounding across the fields, and ran towards her with much leaping and wagging of the tail and other marks of recognition. "Why, Erin! Where did you come from, Erin, and what are you doing here alone?" Margaret looked over the fields to the large white house at the head of the Harbor, where she knew the dog belonged, and saw that the wide, dark-green blinds were closed, and the whole house wore an empty, deserted air. Erin evidently knew all about it; but as he did not tell, they went on together to Captain Nye's, where Mrs. Nye stood waiting on the porch step.

"There, Mis' Temple, I was just telling the Cap'n he'd better go and look for you. Them quahog cakes is just hot and done to a turn; and, says I, Mis' Temple's fell a-dreamin' out in her boat, and you'd better go and look her up, for she does like quahog cakes first-rate."

"That I do, Mrs. Nye. I'll come in this minute; and pray ask the Captain to come and eat his supper with me this evening. I suppose it's of no use to ask you?"

"Why, bless you, no!" exclaimed Mrs. Nye. "And if I did, who in mercy's name's going to mind the cakes? You don't suppose I'd trust 'em to Drushy-Ann, do you? She'd burn 'em to a cinder, or else serve 'em raw as raw. But I'll tell father, and it'll please him clear round. Come along, Erin; you've come for your supper too, I guess."

Margaret found the table covered with good things, of which the quahog cakes were the final expression and flower; and presently in came the Captain, his weather-beaten face and hands shining with soap and water, his best wig on (he had one of a rusty brown for every day, and a lustrous black one for Sunday), and a big, white, starched shirt-collar, the points of which stuck into his eyes at intervals and made him wink. Erin, too, considered himself invited, and stretched himself contentedly at Margaret's feet, asking no questions.

Captain Nye and Margaret were great cronies. She declared there was not one of her male friends from whom she got more solid information and sounder philosophy than from old "Cap'n Bishy," as he was called round about.

"I noticed that the White House was closed, as I came along. What has happened there since last year?"

"You may well ask," replied the Captain. "That house is an eyesore to me whenever I look at it; and it used to be so lively,— what with the human bein's and the dumb critturs. Well, I sometimes tell mother she and I have lived too long. We are about the only things that seem to stand by and not go off out o' Fair Harbor one way or another."

"Tell me about the Sandersons, and why they left the place."

"Well, you see old Squire Sanderson died just after you was here last fall, and poor Mis' Sanderson she almost died herself, grievin' after him. Their only son's away at sea. He's captain of a merchant-vessel, you know, and's mostly away, and they've buried their other children on and off, all but Mary Ann, and she's married and lives over to New Bedford, — married lawyer Doane, a likely young fellow. Mary Ann came to stop with her mother when the Squire died, and seein' her so broken down and lonesome, she just insisted on takin' her back to Bedford. You see 't is quiet here in the winter, and no mistake, and there's a good deal o' stir to Bedford;

so the old lady went, and she's there now, and she's got Mary Ann's baby to pet and play with, and I guess she's considerable consoled. The White House and the barn and all the critturs and fixin's are to let, and I do wish some clever folks would come and take 'em. I promised I'd look after the place and the live-stock until somethin' turned up; and Erin here, he's mostly with us, always at meal-times and at night, though he lies in the sun in front of the White House daytimes, and seems to be waitin' for somebody. It was kind o' cute his knowin' you, was n't it? I don't suppose now," said the Captain, looking at Margaret, — *" I don't suppose — "*

" I'm not at all sure I would n't," said Margaret. *" Can one get into the house to see it ?"*

" Oh, yes, to be sure. I've got the keys in charge, and the whole concern, and I'll take you all over the place any time."

"*To-morrow morning, then,*" said Margaret.

And the next day they did go all over the place; and Margaret (whose principle it was, when you like a thing and want it, take it if you can get it) then and there bought the house and farm and all the belongings, — wagons and farm horses, four good cows (natives crossed with Jersey), and beehives on a settle in the apple-orchard; a vegetable garden behind the house, with a border of twigs for sweet peas to climb on, and plenty of sweet-smelling herbs; in front of the house a flower-garden, with paths divided by high rows of box, where grew guelder roses and calycanthus and Persian lilacs, and all manner of old-fashioned shrubs and flowers. There was a grove of trees on one side, walking down to the water's edge, and the path along the high bank was bordered with sumach and barberry bushes, and whortleberry and bay-

berry and sweet-fern, growing thick and fast, and giving promise of rich color for the autumn-tide. There were broad, green fields for the cows' pleasure-grounds, and high pasture lands where sheep might browse; and the grassy lawn beyond the garden led straight down to the little beach, and to the wharf for boats.

Afterwards, when Captain Nye was talking it over with his wife, he said: " As we were walkin' up to the White House, Mis' Temple says to me, says she, ' Cap'n, I do hope there'll be three kinds of flowers in that garden, — three special kinds that I love, and used to have in a garden of my own when I was a little girl. In fact,' says she, 'if those flowers ain't there, I don't know as I shall take the place.' I was kind o' nervous when she spoke like that, for I did want her to buy; and I was afraid it was some o' them rare things she meant, that they have in gardens, — Mis' May's got some, you know, over to Wood's Holl. High-breds, I believe they call 'em. But there, what do you think, mother? She went into the garden and looked about for a while, and then she said, quite joyful-like, "Oh, here they are, Cap'n, every one!" And she stooped down and made her a little boquay, and put 'em into her dress, and she kissed 'em, and I believe to mercy she cried over 'em some. And what do you think they were? Just ladies' delights,— the little old-fashioned kind, you know,— and striped grass, and 'stars of Bethlehem,' she called 'em."

"Well, well," said Mrs. Nye, "I've given up calculatin' on city folks. They seem to go just contrary to what you'd expect. They don't care for the things you'd figure they'd set by; and then they just go crazy over some little unsignified thing that seemin'ly ain't of no account. I do believe Mis' Temple thinks more of a glass o' new milk and a fresh churnin' o' butter than she does of the best pies and plum-cake and jell that I can set before her. And my last putting up of grape and quince jell was just splendid, if I do say it."

"I shall depend upon you for oysters, Captain," said Margaret. "But quahog cakes! What shall I do for them?"

"Sakes alive!" cried Mrs. Nye, "I'll be bound your city cook'll make 'em much better than me; but you've only to say the word any time, and I'll come over and show her, if she can't."

"That's a bargain," said Margaret. "I know I shall never have such good things, or like my housekeeping as well as yours; but I want to ask some of my friends to come to me in the autumn, and I must have a big house to hold them."

The next morning, before Margaret went back to town, she walked across the fields to view her new possessions. The day was fair, and as delicate-tinted as any opal,— such a day as comes far oftener to our New England coast in spring than its maligners would have the world believe. Margaret's mood was in accord with the time; and as she walked along, her handsome head thrown back, her dark eyes dewy and sweet, her pulses beating time to the song in her heart, her hands full of wild flowers, she made a charming picture. "For spring still makes spring in the mind," says Emerson, who knew the secret of eternal youth. A soft breeze blew from the water, bowing the tall grass and chasing the shadows it made as it ran hither and yon among the fields, and sending great whiffs of perfume from the lilac hedge over the stone wall. The roadside was gay with spring coloring. Red columbines and blue violets; wild geranium and the golden-hearted strawberry blossom; Solomon's seal and anemones, and *that most delicate and gracefullest of vines, the blackberry; the purple-pink fringed polygala; the cassandra, or leather-leaf, holding its white racemes on one side,— they were all here at Margaret's feet, and she took tribute from them all. She crossed a piece of white-sanded beach, and walked up the bank through the little wood at whose edges the shad-blossom and dogwood were in white bloom. There were maple-trees among the pines, clothed in tender shades of red and pale green, waving graceful tassels in the breeze; and oaks trying to make up for lost time, and bud and bourgeon with the rest. "How much red there is in the springtime!" said Margaret. She had the habit, common to those who live alone a good deal, of talking to herself. "Why do people speak as if green were its only wear? Charles d'Orléans knew better when he said,—*

> *'Un premier jour du mois de Mai,
> De tanné et de vert perdu.'*

I never could quite get the right English word for 'tanné,' by the bye,—tan-color *does n't just express it."* She sat down on the soft moss, sprinkled with partridge-berry and wintergreen, and murmured,—

> "The green grass is bowing,
> The morning wind is in it;
> 'T is a tune worth thy knowing,
> Though it change every minute.
> 'T is a tune of the Spring,
> Every year sings it over."

"*Every year sings—sings—*" And Margaret fell into a gentle slumber, and dreamed that she was at home in Boston, and that her sister and brother-in-law were laughing at her terribly for her purchase of the Sanderson estate, and she was getting very angry and very miserable; and then she dreamed that some one stood beside her, and a voice she had not heard for years said earnestly, "It is well; and better than you know remains behind."

A slight noise in the underbrush wakened Margaret, and Erin was by her side, looking at her a little anxiously, until she spoke to him and told him she had not lost her path nor fallen by the way. " I have only had a dream, Erin," she said. So they went on to the White House, Erin marching soberly, with a dignified manner, for he knew he was her natural guide about his old home, and felt the responsibility of the situation.

"*As from some blissful neighborhood
A notice faintly understood,
' I see the end and know the good.'*

"*Like an Æolian harp that wakes
No certain air, but overtakes
Far thought with music that it makes.*

"*Such seemed the whisper at my side.
' What is 't thou know'st, sweet voice?' I cried.
' A hidden hope,' the voice replied.*"

It was October with the heart of May.
E. S. PHELPS.

And round us all the thicket rang,
To many a flute of Arcady.
TENNYSON.

It may be that the gulfs shall wash us down,
It may be we shall touch the Happy Isles.
TENNYSON.

A WEEK AWAY FROM TIME.

FIRST DAY.

"Now, please don't begin with a prejudice, Ralph!"

"My dear Margaret," said Ralph gravely, "I am surprised at you! I thought you knew Latin. If I am to have any prejudices at all (and pray don't attempt to deprive me of them, they are among the few things I have to be proud of), I must begin with them. One cannot end with a prejudice. For the word is formed of two Latin ones, *pre*, signifying—"

"Oh, Ralph, how can you be so provoking!" exclaimed his sister. "I dare say we shall find the girl delightful, and end by all falling in love with her. At any rate, you know I am doing the right thing in asking her to come here. You know how very nice her people were to me in England, and you ought to be glad that I can show any attention to Miss Carr-Wynstede at this season of the year, when no one is in Boston."

"It's so like English people to go there at this season," said Ralph. "And how on earth does she happen to be over here at all? I suppose she is one of those terrible Englishwomen who have lately taken to travelling about in squads, quite able to take care of themselves, *pour cause*, with long pointed noses all ready to sniff, smooth, uncompromising hair taken straight off their brows; long of limb, waterproof as to attire, carrying sketching materials about with them wherever they go,— though never yet have I seen one of them make a picture; utterly unmusical, yet calmly sitting down to the piano unbidden of evenings, and singing English songs as devoid of melody as their voices. I can see them from here."

"I don't know if she sketches, nor how she sings, nor even how she looks. I have never seen her," said Margaret. "When I stayed with her parents in Devonshire, she was away on the Continent — "

"Of course," interjected Ralph, "travelling in a squad, I dare say — "

"With her aunt, Lady Molyneux," went on Margaret, regardless of the interruption; "but I heard of her constantly as a very charming girl, and I shall feel that she is until I find that she is not. And you will be very nice to her, to please me, even if you think her detestable, because you are a great dear, however horrid you may seem."

"That being the case, my ' prepotente ' sister, and having told me how I ought to feel, please tell me what I must do! Am I to drive you to the station to meet this young woman with two names, — for I believe she is to arrive this afternoon, — and by which name shall I look for her?"

"Listen," said Margaret, "to a letter I had this morning from Bell, who, wonderful to relate, is going to rouse herself sufficiently to come to this despised spot after a summer at Bar Harbor."

Margaret took a letter from the table and read: —

BOSTON, Saturday, September 29.

YOU DEAR UTOPIAN, — I can conceive of nothing more incongruous, more absolutely untoward, than the presence of that English girl with the two names (Tom calls her the two-headed girl) in the midst of our family party for a whole week, and — Heaven save the mark! — at Cape Cod! ["There! you see!" grumbled Ralph.] But since you will have it so, and since, I confess, whatever you undertake in this line is apt to turn out well, I will do your bidding, — call upon General and Mrs. Carr-Wynstede at the Brunswick Hotel on Monday, be presented to the daughter, and bear her away with me to lunch. See how I love you! — a call on strangers at high noon, for me, who hate both strangers and high noon, and a long journey by rail of nearly two hours; all in one day! ["'Nearly two hours'! Hear her!" said Margaret, "and by the 'Flying Dude'!"] Nevertheless, it shall be done. So expect us by the afternoon train. I have no idea where I am going, nor how we get there; but Tom knows, and he will engineer us. The children are both away, — Dick in the Adirondacks, with some of his "fellows," and your namesake, Peggy, Tom took to his mother's, at Oaklands, yesterday. As she went away she said, "I wish I were going with you to aunty, mamma;

grandma is very nice and kind, but she is n't aunty—nobody is!" I shall not bring my maid, thanks, for I am sure your Susan will do all I want for me (you say Miss C.-W. takes a French maid with her), but I will bring Joujou, if you don't mind. He would die of grief if he were left behind, and so should I. By the bye, Charlie Wyatt came to see us last evening. He says his yacht, the "Hope," is not laid up yet, and that he shall take her round to Fair Harbor and put her and himself at your service. I said it must be too cold to sail (and at any rate nothing would drag *me* on board a boat, you know), but he said, "Too cold at the Cape! The first week in October! Oh dear! no. It will be perfect sailing weather, and a full moon!" He has the Cape madness as badly as you and Ralph, so I did n't discuss with him. He looked bored, and twirled his long golden moustache a good deal (I declare he is handsomer than ever) when I told him of Miss C.-W.; and I tried to cheer him by saying perhaps she did n't like yachting any better than I. "They do, they all like it!" said he gloomily. "Look at Lady Brassey! I dare say this one will be taking the helm and ordering my men about. But to please dear Mrs. Temple I would take Queen Victoria herself on a cruise!" He certainly could n't say fairer than that, could he? Till Monday afternoon, then, and with love from Tom, Your sister,

BELL BOWDOIN.

P. S. I was going to take down quantities of eatables, —*pâtés de foie gras* and French canned things,— but Tom says you'd be insulted; that you disapprove of *foie gras* on humane grounds, because it hurts the geese,— not the geese who eat, but those who are eaten,— and that you are not camping out on a desert island. Still, I notice he has a hamper of pears and hot-house grapes in the hall addressed to you. I suppose even you will acknowledge that there are neither vines nor fig-trees in your Paradise. And yet, I am not so sure.

P. S. 2d. So you really mean to put us all under contribution for something to amuse our evenings! Tom vows he never wrote anything in his life but checks to pay my bills. As for me, I have had no time at Mount Desert for anything so serious as writing a story. But perhaps I may cudgel my brains one day down there while you are all out in that dreadful boat, and beat up a trifle of some sort. We shall see.

"I am sorry Tom discouraged Bell's good intentions in the commissariat department," said

A Week away from Time. 37

Ralph. "I have a tremendous appetite, having positively eaten nothing in New York for weeks. This air makes one ravenous. I think I devoured a bushel of oysters at luncheon. You've got a capital cook, Margaret. Is she a native?"

"No," said Margaret. "Don't tell Bell and Tom; they will laugh at me. You know how I have always praised the cooking here; and certainly when I have been at Captain Nye's, and dear Mrs. Nye superintended everything, it left nothing to be desired. She used to get what she called an 'abrigoine' from Marshpee to help her, you know; and somehow when the Red Indian was under her influence she did excellently well. But I have not been fortunate in my experiences with the original owners of the soil; I got one from Marshpee when I first came to the White House in September. She was really a very good cook, and I thought we should never part."

"Well, what happened? Did her proud spirit refuse to accept a hireling's pay, or did you send her for a scholarship to Hampton?"

"Neither," replied Margaret laughing. "But the first time I paid her her wages she departed, going back to her native wigwam, and, I regret to say, taking all the week's family wash with her. I forbore to prosecute her, in view of the wrongs of the Indian race. So I called it quits — got some more table linen, and a cook from Boston. But it is time for you to drive to the station. I told Bell to get out at Wood's Holl rather than Falmouth, the drive thence is so pretty. Tell David to put the bays into the beach-wagon for you, and he can go himself for Miss Carr-Wynstede's maid. I do feel a little nervous about the French maid, I confess. I am afraid we shan't be able to amuse her. Let Erin run along with you and be introduced to his cousin Joujou."

Ralph sighed deeply. "We were so happy here, — we two!" he said. "When I think of our Arcadia being invaded by unsympathetic relatives (unsympathetic to the beauties of Fair Harbor, I mean) and by the British female, — when I think that we are all expected to write stories and read them aloud of evenings just as they do in books, but never in real life that I ever heard of, — it really does seem, Margaret, like voluntarily introducing the serpent into our Eden, and I only hope he will not turn and rend us! How many shall we be in all?"

"With Mr. Wyatt, whom I count as a guest, and to whom I have sent word that he must bring a story, — poor fellow! — we shall be six," said Margaret.

"Don't you think we had better be seven and done with it? It is a magic number, and besides, it just fills out the days of the week. Whom else shall we have? Did you know that Philip Kirkland had got home from Europe — Japan — India — Heaven knows where? I met him in Boston the day I came down here. He asked for you, and I wanted to tell him then to take the train and come and see how you are, but I did n't quite know. How long is it since you saw him?"

Margaret had risen while Ralph was speaking, and walked to the open window, where she stood breaking off branches of pink and white honeysuckle from a vine which grew from the porch across the casement, in a quick, nervous way. She answered her brother without turning her head.

"How long? I don't quite remember. It is several years. We were in Rome, you know."

"Why don't you send for him?" said Ralph cheerfully. "He is out and out the most interesting man I know, and no end of a good fellow. Write a line now, asking him to come down to-morrow afternoon, and I'll take it to the mail myself. I will go to the stable and come back for your note. He can telegraph his answer." And he left the house and was out of sight before Margaret turned round. When she did, her face was flushed and her eyes were shining with some unwonted emotion.

"How foolish I am!" she said aloud. "I am sure he has forgotten. I dare say I imagined it then. Is it all because of that dream of mine in the woods last spring? Shall I be governed by a dream of the springtime, — I, for whom it is no longer spring? No. I will ask him, and we shall meet like any other good friends who have not met for years and who sincerely like each other. I dare say he won't even care to come, he has been at home so little while."

When Ralph returned, driving the bays to the door, Margaret stood in the porch, the note in her hand and the flush faded from her cheek. When he had gone, she took her scissors and went into the garden to cut fresh flowers for her guests' bedrooms, singing to herself, —

"What's the way to Arcady, — to Arcady?"

Italy, my Italy!
Queen Mary's saying serves for me; —
Open my heart and you will see
  Graved inside of it, " Italy."
Such lovers of old are I and she —
So it always was, so it still shall be.

ROBERT BROWNING.

EVENING OF FIRST DAY.

"IT is really very nice here, — far nicer than I thought," said Mrs. Bowdoin. "You never told me how beautiful the view is coming from Wood's Holl, where one looks down upon Buzzard's Bay on one side and Vineyard Sound on the other, and upon those miles and miles of rolling wooded country."

"I have told you a thousand times," said Margaret.

"And why did you never say how enchanting the little harbor is when one turns the corner of the lane yonder and comes upon it so unexpectedly? I fairly screamed with delight."

"I have said it constantly for years," replied Margaret.

"As to the air, — and I confess I *have* heard you speak of the air, — I never felt anything so delicious. It is as soft as Newport, with a hundred times more snap to it. It has quite gone to my head. And the house," she went on as Margaret showed her upstairs to her room, — " how charming it is, with the big hall, and the white wainscoting, and the wide staircase with carved balusters, and this landing with a window-seat, and such a lovely view! And oh, Margaret, what big, sunny, cheerful rooms! You could n't have had anything better if you had built it yourself."

"Nothing half as good," said Margaret, "for this was built nearly a hundred years ago."

Presently, when the brothers and sisters were sitting together in the large, comfortable room on the right of the hall door which Margaret had made into her library, waiting for Miss Carr-Wynstede to come downstairs to afternoon tea, "Well, how did you find her? What do you think of her?" asked Margaret eagerly, turning first to one and then to the other. "She is certainly very handsome; that I could see for myself."

"I know Tom and Ralph are just dying to speak," said Mrs. Bowdoin, "but I insist upon the floor."

A Week away from Time. 47

"As if she did n't always have the floor!" said her husband. "I am not even allowed in the chair to keep order. However, I have my views of the young lady, which I shall take a grim pleasure in keeping to myself."

"You may as well," retorted his wife. "They will be of no benefit to any one else. You were n't at home at lunch, and you passed your time on the way down in the smoking-car, shamelessly, with your boon companions from those two dens of crime up the Bay, the Monumental and Forefathers Clubs. And you and Ralph hardly addressed a word to either Miss Carr-Wynstede or me on the drive here. I am the only person who can tell you anything about her."

"I am waiting," said Margaret. "But be quick, for she will be coming down soon. I left Susan struggling to make Marie understand the lay of the land upstairs. Miss Carr-Wynstede told me Marie was very anxious to learn English, so I did n't attempt to interpret for her. Go on, Bell."

"To begin with, then," said Mrs. Bowdoin,

"must we always call her by her two names? It is such a bore, and takes so long. One can abbreviate in writing, but one can't call her Miss C.-W. to her face. Why will English people be so absurd? Life is not long enough for hyphens. What is her Christian name, I wonder?"

"Muriel," said Mrs. Temple. "She sent me a charming note in answer to my invitation (for I wrote to her separately when I learned that her parents could not come), and it was signed 'Muriel.'"

"How English, to be sure! Such an out-of-the-way name! But I must say I like it. It is my only reason for regretting that I was not born English; then I might have been Gwendolyn, or Gladys, or Iseult. Don't smile in that aggravating way, Tom! I feel just like Iseult. Very well," she continued; "I went to the Brunswick and paid my call on the father and mother. They were very nice, I must say, Margaret, and they said charming things of you, and how much they cared for you. And as we were talking, and they were saying how sorry they were their engagements prevented their passing the week with you, and how glad they were to confide their daughter to my care, and all that, the young lady herself came into the room. I confess I was unprepared for such beauty; she really is exquisitely lovely. I took her home with me, and we got on very well. She did n't talk much; I can't tell if it is shyness, or want of anything to say."

"I think I could explain it," remarked Mr. Bowdoin dryly; "it is for the same reason that I am a small talker at home. One thing I will reveal; when the young lady got out of the wagon just now, I saw an uncommonly pretty little foot, which was more — or rather less — than I expected. Did you notice it, Ralph?"

"And what a beautiful voice she has!" exclaimed Margaret, — "low and sweet and clear. I could fall in love with a voice like that if I were a man."

"It seems to be the classical voice with nothing beside, as far as I can make out," said Ralph. "You have spent the day with the girl, Bell, and you have told us nothing about her except that she is good-looking, which we can see for ourselves. I don't believe there is much to tell. I believe I know just what sort of person she is: she rides and hunts and plays lawn tennis. Oh, yes, of course she plays lawn tennis! I am so thankful Margaret has no tennis-court. Don't pray be having one marked out in the sand on the beach! Let her see that there is one spot on the earth where sensible people can get along without that assertive and all-pervading game. And she takes long walks, and cares more for horses and dogs than for any human being; and when she wants to express the highest praise of any one, she calls him or her 'doggy'! *Why* Margaret insisted upon asking her! It's going to be a horrid nuisance."

At this moment a rustle was heard on the stairs, and in another the English girl stood at the door of the library. There was one awkward moment, for the whole party felt guilty and ashamed of themselves to have been discussing their guest so freely, and then Mrs. Temple went forward and took her hand and spoke in her own cordial, sweet way, which always made strangers feel quite at home directly.

"When we have had a cup of tea," she said, "if you are not too tired we will walk toward the headlands yonder and see the sun set over the water; that is what one cannot often witness on our eastern coast."

"Indeed, I am not in the least tired," said Miss Carr-Wynstede, "and I meant to ask if I might take a walk. But please don't trouble yourself to come with me. I'd much rather find my way alone, if I may take your handsome setter with me. Oh, I don't really mean that I'd rather go alone, you know, only — I thought — I —" And the poor girl flushed crimson, and looked so troubled that Margaret pitied her.

"Hullo!" cried out Mr. Bowdoin, who was standing at the hall door looking out, — " Hullo! here's a yacht coming into the harbor, a sloop. I truly believe it is the 'Hope.' Wyatt has been as good as his word. Now, Miss Carr-Wynstede, you will see our handsome man, our Antinous, our champion ' masher;' and the queer part of it is, he's an awfully good fellow."

"Let us all go down to the pier to see the 'Hope' come in," said Margaret; "and you shall have Erin for your special escort, my dear," turning to Muriel with a charming smile.

Mrs. Bowdoin said she could see both the sunset and the yacht very well from the porch. Margaret and Mr. Bowdoin walked together, so Ralph was obliged to be the English girl's companion; but he was really quite embarrassed and awkward, for he felt that she had probably heard what he was saying when she came downstairs. So they walked silently through the garden, sweet with the scent of late roses, heliotrope, and mignonette; along the path cut through a tangle of golden-rod, bayberry, grapevines, and purple asters, till they came down to the wharf just as the "Hope" reached moorings and the gig was pushing off with her handsome captain. He raised his cap in answer to waving handkerchiefs, and in a few minutes he had shaken hands heartily with his friends and had been presented to Miss Carr-Wynstede. Mr. Bowdoin had spoken truly; he really was as handsome as it is given to man to be. The sun and the sea-air had tanned his almost too fair skin to a rich brown, and as he stood with his yachtsman's cap in his hand, in his yachtsman's dress, more than six feet of broad-shouldered vigorous manhood, his yellow moustache glowing in the setting sun's rays with every shade of tawny gold, his blue eyes, — blue as violets are blue, — sometimes rather sleepy, and half veiled by heavy lashes, but now lighted with honest, frank pleasure, Charlie Wyatt was the very picture of a sun-god in uniform.

"Here I am, dear Mrs. Temple, and here is my boat; and both are yours, to use or abuse, as pleases you. You must look upon us as a part of your establishment, but you must never let either of us bore you."

"I want to see Captain Nye about a new centre-board for your cat-boat, Margaret," said Ralph. "I'll be at home in time to dress for dinner."

So when the party went back to the house, the last rays of the sun fell upon Wyatt walking by Miss Carr-Wynstede, looking down into her face with those blue eyes which he had found very troublesome many times in his life, so much more had been understood from them than he had ever intended to convey. Margaret whispered to her brother-in-law, "Oh, dear! I hope she won't go to falling in love with him and breaking her heart. I wish he were n't so ridiculously handsome; and he's as unsusceptible as he is beautiful."

After dinner, when the men had had their cigarettes and the ladies had sat for half an hour in the broad porch giving themselves up to enjoyment of the moonlight and the soft, odor-laden air as it came from the sea across the flowers, Margaret said, "It is really too bad to go into the house and leave all this loveliness; but I mean to be stern about this thing, and we must begin to-night, or we never shall. I shall set you a good example, but this evening's entertainment will be a mild one. I shall read you a letter I have lately received from my dear friend Mr. Johns, who is in Italy. It is about Beatrice Bernardi, the peasant Improvisatrice, whom we know of through the 'Roadside Songs of Tuscany,' of 'Francesca,' which have been edited and so greatly admired by Mr. Ruskin. The letter describes a visit paid to Beatrice by Mr. and Mrs. Johns."

"It is a shame to go in," said Wyatt, in a low voice to Miss Carr-Wynstede. "One does n't have many evenings like this, even at Fair Harbor."

Just then a figure appeared at the open window of a room above where they stood.

"Oh, Marie, don't close the shutters, please!" said Miss Carr-Wynstede. "I like to have the moonlight in my room."

"Is that your room?" asked Wyatt. "Then when you see the 'Hope's' light shining yonder, won't you think that it is burning for you, and keeping watch for you while you sleep?"

When the company had seated themselves in the library to their satisfaction, Wyatt securing to himself a chair behind Miss Carr-Wynstede, Margaret began: —

<small>CUTIGLIANO, APPENNINO PISTOJESE, Aug. 15, 188–.</small>

MY DEAR MARGARET, — E. and I went to-day to see Beatrice. Beatrice Bernardi is the most remarkable of the Improvisatori, male or female, who have been in Italy during the last sixty years. She was born in the neighborhood of Cutigliano about eighty years ago. Her parents were poor, as are all the peasants of these mountains. She had no instruction, and to-day does not know how to read or write; but she always delighted in Nature, and used to sing to herself about the flowers and the trees and the sunlight and the sky as she tended the sheep or worked in the fields or gathered the chestnuts. At twenty she married, and the first "ottava"[1] she ever sang (her first improvisation) as it were aloud, was to her husband on their wedding-day. Here in their mountains, which the poet Tommaseo calls "the most poetic place in the poetic Tuscan land," poetry is to these poor mountaineers a necessity, and the fame of Beatrice soon spread. From that time forward she sang constantly, and with such effect that her fame was carried all abroad, so that she was sent for by rich and distinguished persons to sing for them, and among the people she always collected a great crowd whenever she sang. Thus she went to Bologna, Pistoja, and Florence. Manzoni sent

---

[1] An "ottava" is a poetical stanza of eight verses of eleven syllables, of which the first six rhyme alternately and the last two rhyme with each other.

for her to come to Milan to see him, but died before she could start. Tommaseo and Giuliani went to see her frequently, and the former began his collection of popular poesy by songs taken from her lips. "Here, for the first time," says he, "I felt the popular poesy revealed to me by Beatrice on the mountains, in its modest beauty, opening for me a new life; whence the Lima is more memorable to me than the Arno."

And so her fame increased, and she went from place to place singing, always to the enthusiastic delight of hundreds. When she once warmed up, she could go on singing for hours. "I could sing all day long, and all night too, when I was young," she told us. Other Improvisatori challenged her, and many were the tournaments; but she defeated them all, and put many vain ones to shame, so that finally all acknowledged her supremacy. Meanwhile she became the mother of ten children, of whom five are dead, as is her husband. She has always retained her mountain home, and there she lives, with two of her sons and their families, the life of a peasant, — this woman who has known most of the distinguished literary men of Italy of her day. Although eighty years old, she still walks over the stony paths of the mountain to Cutigliano, three hours away. Many strangers go to see her, and she is the great personage of "the Mountain."

So E. and I went to see Beatrice. E. went on a donkey — or thought she did — and I walked. The donkey was small and of much character. Her name was Margherita, in compliment to Italy's attractive and beloved queen. This donkey had two devilish proclivities: one was an almost invincible indisposition to be mounted; the other, a strong objection to going when she was mounted. She also had a way of puffing herself out while the saddle was being girthed, and of drawing herself in at different points on the road, so that the very ugly and very awkward saddle was slipping round most frequently and inopportunely. This gave my beloved companion the privilege of walking one half or more of the way, to the evident satisfaction of the female owner of the donkey, our guide, who looked as if she thought stout strangers ought to carry small donkeys, and pay well for the chance; for on the plea that she had had twelve children, seven of whom were dead, this person had, of course, extracted from my companion the promise to pay double the usual price, and her only object now was to get through the job with as little fatigue and inconvenience to the donkey as possible. So our ears were regaled with accounts of the fondness of the children (living and dead) for Margherita; of the beauty and delicacy of her feet, and of her dislike of stony roads (now, all roads in this part of the country are stony, and this road the stoniest I ever saw out of Palestine); of our good fortune in having secured the donkey, which two foreign parties had sought in vain to do after we had hired her; with no end of more lies, which E. thought all right because the woman had chosen to have twelve children and had lost seven of them. I confess to much ill-humor in being kept back by this lazy beast, who should have been well thrashed; but the delay was of no account, for had not her owner had twelve children, and seven of them were dead, and they were all fond of the donkey? Men are brutes; and women — well, some are tender-hearted and some cunning. The road climbs the side of the mountain to Pian degli Ontani under the chestnut-trees. Far below rushes the Sestajone, just about to join the Lima, over its torrent bed, making gleams of silver and white through the sparkling leaves of the chestnuts. At intervals little clear brooks cross the stony path, hurrying down to join the larger stream; and every now and then we came to the smothering, smoking, black-brown piles in which the charcoal was being burned, and which gave out strong odors of pyroligneous acid.

Just before we arrived at Pian degli Ontani — a village of a church and about twenty houses — we came to a little pool of clear bright water, so small that it could scarcely have harbored a dozen ducks. It was shaded by great chestnut-trees, and was quite a pretty spot. "See that tiny, lovely, bright little water," said our guide in those caressing diminutives in which the Italian language abounds. "There a 'bella sposina' (a pretty little wife) drowned herself a few months ago. She was only twenty-two, and left a little one only a few months old."

"But why?"

"Oh, she was not happy. Her mother had made her marry a young man whom she did not love. She told her mother she would drown herself some day. She had been married only two years."

"Did she love some one else?" asked we, with that universal idea that if a woman does n't love one man she must love another.

"Oh, no! She did not love any one else."

"Was the husband old, or cross, or violent?"

"Oh, no! He was young. He had been in love with her for years. Nobody could tell why she did it. She told her mother she would do it some day. Her husband got up early in the morning to go to his charcoal-burning, and soon after she got up, and in her night-clothes, with only a petticoat on, she left her baby on the bed; she went down there, and kept her head under the water until she was dead."

"But she must have been 'pazza' (crazy)."

"No, she was not 'pazza.' She always told her mother she would do it. Poor sposina! Yes — she left her baby on the bed and went there and drowned herself." As we went through the village, there were three men lounging by the fountain in that easy way in which Italian peasants always astonish us by their grace. After we had passed them, our guide said, —

"Did you see that young man nearest to the fountain? He was the husband, 'poverino!' Yes, he was the husband."

He was a handsome young fellow. Had she told us that some romantic girl had drowned herself because he would not marry her, we should have been less surprised.

"Speriamo! Let us hope that he and the mother-in-law may be able to console each other!" said the mother of twelve children.

From Pian degli Ontani to Pian di Novello, where Beatrice now lives, the road still mounts, although not quite so rapidly. The chestnuts became mingled with beeches — curiously twisted old beeches — and young birches with bright fresh leaves and silver trunks with dark patches on them. The steep mountain-sides were in many places covered with them, in others bare and stony, with great chasms worn by rushing rains. In the distance the peaks were shining in the sunlight with beautiful variety of color, throwing off the light instead of absorbing it, as in painting on porcelain. Wild flowers and delicate heather abounded, and little patches of yellow grain on terraces gilded the landscape. Down below, by the side of the fast running stream, was a group of mill-buildings, and the sound of the clapper and of barking dogs mounted up to us. And so on for nearly an hour and a half after we had left Pian degli Ontani. At last we arrived before the little stone house shaded by a tall cherry-tree. There was a stable close by, and piled around it were sheaves of yellow grain just brought in from the terraced fields. Two young women, her daughters-in-law, met us at the door, and in an instant appeared on the threshold Beatrice herself, with as many affectionate greetings as if we had been old friends and she had been expecting us for months. "Why, how do their worships do? I am so glad to see them! Come in, come in. I am so glad to see them! Let them take the trouble to sit down. I am *so* glad to see them!"

We sat down and looked at her. The first thing that struck us was the wonderful brightness of her handsome eyes, the refinement of her looks and motions and manners. She is a very handsome old woman, —

a handsome brow, beautiful eyes, delicate nose, well-formed and expressive mouth; none of the coarseness which one might expect in an old peasant who had spent her life in the Apennine Mountains, worked hard, and lived principally on chestnuts. None of the photographs I have seen of her do her any justice. It is difficult to recall everything she said, and impossible to recall it *as* she said it. E. had brought her some kerchiefs such as the peasants wear on their heads and shoulders; one of silk, two of cotton, and a warmer one of wool, — inexpensive trifles, but of bright, gay colors. She thanked us with warmth, but did not open them, nor show any vulgar curiosity, but sat with them folded on her lap during our visit. She talked constantly. Her voice was very pleasing. She told us of the people who had come to see her, of the illustrious literary men she had known, of the places she had visited. She had been to Florence, to Bologna and Pistoja, and to many other cities. And she had been all over the mountains, yes, all over. A beautiful countess from Venice had been to see her and had told her all about that city of the sea. People had come from England, and even America. She had been sent for by Manzoni, and was to have gone to Milan, — yes, all the way to Milan, — when he died, " povero ! " and she did not go. Had we ever heard of Manzoni?

He was a famous writer. She did not read herself, nor write, but people read to her. Had we heard of Manzoni? "Oh! yes, we had heard of him."

"Davvero! (indeed!)" Well, she was to have gone to see him, at his request, and he died and she did not go. "Povero! he died. And I knew Tommaseo, who used to listen to me hour after hour, and wrote down what I said. And I knew Giuliani, who wrote letters to Tommaseo about me, and printed them in a book."

"Yes, we have read the book."

"Davvero! Yes, men had been for hours and days writing down all that I said and improvised and recited, — 'ottave' and 'stornelli' and 'rispetti.' I have sung and recited everywhere. No other Improvisatori could compete with me. I have had many trials with them, and I have conquered them all, — yes, all — men and women. One man quite lost his voice singing against me, and never got it back. When I once got started I could go on almost forever. The verses poured out like water from a fountain."

"You have had a happy life. We know that you have had sorrows, but still your life has been a happy one."

"Chè! *chè!* CHÈ! CHÈ!" These four *chè's* in crescendo were inimitable. "I think I *have* been happy. E altro!" She beamed all over, and you might have thought she had never known a care in her life. We remembered the death of her son, the destruction of her house at Pian degli Ontani by the flood which swept it to the river, the pain and trouble of building the very house in which we were seated, for which she carried all the stones up the hill, until her "reins were sore," as she had said to Giuliani. But for the moment she had forgotten all this. I asked her how old she was. "If it please the Lord Jesus Christ to spare me, I shall be eighty next March." She speaks the purest Tuscan, and the words roll out to one's delight. I asked her, with intention, if she did not sing or recite or improvise now. She said, "Oh! I am too old. My voice is all gone — see!" And then she began to sing, with a voice so pure and musical, although, of course, weakened by age, that it astonished us. It was as if she had taken the note from some rich-voiced bird's warbling. She sang a number of verses in that Oriental way which Spanish gypsies and Egyptian almées had made familiar to us. It was startling to hear in these Italian mountains strains which in their form we thought belonged only to Moors and Arabs. "Does that please you?" She was evidently delighted with the wonder and pleasure she saw depicted in our faces. And she began to recite some "ottave" with a smoothness of rhythm and correctness of measure that could not be excelled. Then, warming up, she began "rispetti"[1] on the creation of the world, following them with improvised verses wonderful to hear. I remembered what Tommasco had written: "At Cutigliano I have found a rich vein of song which has required many days to exhaust. A certain Beatrice, wife of a shepherd, who knew not how to write, but who could improvise wonderfully, — a woman about thirty years old, with an inspired flash of the eye;" and I thought of Giuliani's enthusiastic words: "Words cannot express to you the astonishment which fills my mind. I have at last had the delight to see the admirable Beatrice of Pian degli Ontani, and to listen to her sweet improvisation, incredible to those who have never heard it. She is really a prodigy of Nature. Her verse overflows with clearness and breadth, is ever abundant and never failing. And what ingenuity of sentiment ever accompanies it! What life and grace of expression! What truth of feeling! An entirely new thing is this woman, who by a divine instinct reveals and expands herself in giving forth poetry while she is tending cattle; who

---

[1] Short compositions of one or two stanzas, which are generally on amatory subjects, sung and composed by the contadini themselves.

knows nothing of letters, and lives separated from fellowship with the world. In ancient Greece she surely would have been numbered among the singers selected upon earth to emulate the muses and to give perpetual delight to men."

All this, and more, came to our minds as we listened to one after the other of the verses she poured forth. I recognized some lines which Giuliani had written down and printed: —

> "E gran sollago ci verremo a dare,
> Che di scrittura non posso imparare;
> La Montagna è stata di noi maestra,
> La Natura ci venne a nutricare," —

which give an idea of the happy thoughts which inspire her. After a time she burst forth into an improvisation of which we were the subject. She thanked us in rich and smooth verse for all our kindness. She asked the good God — "the good God who made the noble trees and the beautiful flowers and the singing birds and the rich sunshine" — to bless us with all His best things. She sang of our having come across the sea to visit her. She thanked us again, and wound up with a new burst of blessings. We remarked upon the beauty of the surroundings, — the mountains and their varied forms and colors, the great trees and their beautiful green, the river in its rocky bed, the golden grain-patches, the lights and shadows and floating clouds, and the marvellous blue sky over all. She had seen and felt it all, and spoke of it all as would a poet, with the fullest appreciation of the beauty and blessing of its loveliness.

Time had flown, and we had to go. There was a long walk, and there was Margherita of the tender feet. Beatrice offered us fresh milk, and then came the adieux, which were as cordial as if we had known each other all our lives. She said she would be glad to go to Cutigliano to see us, but she was so old! (She subsequently came, and walked all the way.) At last the good-byes were said, and we started on our return. My companion walked half the way, to the mother of twelve children's delight, and rode the balance, to my satisfaction. We reached home just at dusk. As we approached the village, the husband of the mother of the twelve, carrying the youngest in his arms, and followed by all the survivors, came in procession to meet the donkey and to escort us, with many smiles and exclamations, chiefly addressed to Margherita. Nearing the stable, the mother of her children pointed out the "stalla" of the donkey, with strong hints and many allusions to tender feet. My tender-hearted was humbugged by the cunning one, and another was added to the victims of craft. The donkey walked into her "stalla," and no doubt chuckled with her mistress over the simplicity of the "forestieri."

The following day a visitor was announced, and appeared in the shape of a pretty granddaughter of Beatrice, aged about eighteen. She came to bring us a basket of wild strawberries gathered on the mountain, and another of black cherries, with loving messages from her grandmother. We asked her if she were the grandchild who had inherited the voice of Beatrice. She acknowledged that she was, but we could not overcome her shyness and persuade her to sing. After a little time another visitor was announced, and she fled with her empty baskets, carrying many messages to that rare old woman, the peer of whom has not been known, at least within the last sixty years, as an Improvisatrice. I know that you will be interested in this account of her, my dear Margaret, and I remain, etc.

"What a simple, delightful story the letter tells, does it not," said Mrs. Temple, " and how thoroughly it has the Italian spirit and local flavor! Have you been in Italy, Miss Carr-Wynstede?"

"Yes," was the answer; "I was in Italy for three years."

"Ah! then you have doubtless heard 'stornelli' and 'rispetti' in their own land. Mr. Wyatt, do sing to us some of your Italian national songs. I trust you have your banjo with you?"

"It is on board my boat; I cannot deny it. I will whistle for it, if you say so."

"For this evening my guitar will do," said Margaret, "and you can begin with 'E quando per udir la predica.'"

Charlie Wyatt took the guitar and sang one song after the other, easily, gracefully, in a rich, mellow barytone. While he was singing, Miss Carr-Wynstede rose from her chair, walked out of the room, — out of the house, — and they could see her tall, slender figure standing in the moonlight in her white dress, her head slightly bent, like a lily on its stalk, leaning against the vine-covered porch.

"She's a calm young woman," muttered Ralph to himself. "I suppose singing bores her."

A Week away from Time. 71

When Wyatt had stopped, she came back.

"Do you sing?" asked Mrs. Bowdoin.

"Yes, I sing," said the girl, and her voice trembled slightly.

"Will you sing?" said Wyatt eagerly, bearing her no grudge for her apparent indifference to his own music.

"Not to-night, please," she replied.

When Wyatt rose to go, Mrs. Temple said, —

"You know I should be only too glad to have you stay here, but I suppose I cannot induce you to sleep on land. You must do everything but sleep here, though. Come to breakfast to-morrow, and we will arrange our day."

When Muriel looked out of her window that night, the moon was high in the heavens, and the "Hope's" light burned steadily as she lay at her moorings just across the harbor, as if it were burning only for her to see.

*Oh, good gigantic smile o' the brown old earth,
This autumn morning! How he sets his bones
To bask i' the sun, and thrusts out knees and feet
For the ripple to run over in its mirth;
Listening the while, where on the heap of stones
The white breast of the sea-lark twitters sweet.*
ROBERT BROWNING.

*High grace, the dower of queens; and there withal
Some wood-born wonder's sweet simplicity:
A glance like water brimming with the sky,
Or hyacinth-light where forest shadows fall:
Such thrilling pallor of cheek as doth enthrall
The heart; a mouth whose passionate forms imply
All music and all silence held thereby:
Deep golden locks, her sovereign coronal.*
DANTE GABRIEL ROSSETTI.

SECOND DAY.

THERE were two big linden-trees near the house, which had been planted there in old Squire Sanderson's boyhood; and under them Mrs. Temple had a table covered with books and magazines, a Scheveningen chair, Persian rugs, and various seats and cushions. A parrot which Margaret had brought from Europe years ago hung in his cage from one of the branches, and a hammock swung between the trees, which Mrs. Bowdoin took possession of on Tuesday morning, and announced her intention of not leaving through the entire week.

"You promised me hammock weather in this famous climate;" she exclaimed, "and please don't ask me to do things! I hate doing things. I was bored to death at Bar Harbor by being constantly obliged to go on all sorts of dreadful excursions. One had to go, or be disliked. Let me alone here, please; it's all I ask. I shall not mind if you go away and leave me. Of course, Margaret will be wanting to show the beauties of her beloved Cape to Miss Carr-Wynstede; Polly and I can talk to one another, and I can listen to the wind whispering in the pine-trees yonder, and to the lapping of the waves on the beach below. I shall be quite happy."

"The 'Hope' is just hoisting sail, you see," said Charlie Wyatt. "She is at your disposition whenever you command, Mrs. Temple."

"Thanks," replied Margaret. "I believe she must content herself with a masculine party to-day. I am going to take Miss Carr-Wynstede to drive presently, when we have been to call on Mrs. Nye, and Bell seems to have arranged herself for the morning. She wishes to be left alone for purposes of composition, I presume. You can take Ralph and Tom with you, Mr. Wyatt; only don't sail away too far! We lunch at two, you know."

Wyatt looked a little disappointed, but only asked, "How is Miss Carr-Wynstede this morning?"

"Very well," replied Margaret. "I left her writing letters in her room. I wish to say, here and now, that she has won my heart; that I find her absolutely lovely. I don't think I ever met a girl who more completely captivated me on first acquaintance."

"Whew! Margaret," cried Ralph, "what a pace you do go at, when you once get started! What has the 'Engländerin' done or said to fetch you like that? And pray when did she do or say it? In the night-watches, when the rest of us were slumbering, all unconscious of this conqueror come among us?"

"Yes, you have guessed," answered Margaret quietly. "In the night-watches. You have said it. Last night, as I was sitting by the fire in my bedroom, there was a gentle knock at the door, and when it was opened, Miss Carr-Wynstede stood, hesitating a little, and said, ' I beg your pardon, Mrs. Temple, but may I come in for a moment?' I cannot tell you how lovely she looked, in a long, softly-falling white peignoir, her golden hair gathered into a great loose coil, setting off the perfect shape of her head and throat, as the open sleeves of her dress showed arms and hands of rare shape and fairness. As she came forward to speak to me, I looked into her beautiful eyes, and thought I saw traces of recent tears. 'What is it, my dear girl?' I said. 'Are you ill? Has anything happened to trouble you?' I made her sit down by me, and she said, 'Dear Mrs. Temple, what must you think of me? Indeed, I know I have been very tiresome and very stupid, but I never meant to be rude; and yet twice in these few hours I must have seemed so.' I took her hands in mine, and tried to say that I did not know what she meant; but she went on: 'When I first came downstairs this afternoon (I am going to tell you the exact truth, Mrs. Temple) I caught a few words which your brother was saying, and they made me feel shy and embarrassed.'"

Here Ralph colored violently, and Polly, who was tired of receiving no attention, screamed out, "I told you so! I told you so!"

"'It was very foolish of me to show anything,' she continued, 'but I had feared that it must be a great bore to have a stranger in your little circle, and now I was sure of it. That was why I said I would rather take the dog, and walk by myself. But it was very tiresome of me. I beg your pardon. I am awfully ashamed of myself.'"

["I wonder how Ralph feels about it?" whispered Tom Bowdoin to his wife.

"Not very happy, I should say, judging from the vicious way in which he is knocking the heads off those poor white daisies."]

"I assured her that we had none of us noticed anything amiss in her, and that it was for *us* to be mortified and shocked (as indeed I was and am) that we should have been so ill-mannered as to have been discussing her at all. 'Then, when Mr. Wyatt was singing,' she said, 'what must he, what must you have thought? But if you knew, dear Mrs. Temple, what his songs reminded me of! My only sister and I were in Italy together. We used to sing all those songs.' She stopped for a moment; her eyes filled and her voice shook as she added simply, 'My sister died in Florence. We both loved Italy passionately. That beautiful letter had brought it all back to me, and I was afraid I should burst into tears if I stayed in the room. But I suppose Mr. Wyatt will never sing for me again.' We talked for a long time," said Margaret, " and, as I tell you, she won my heart forever. And I think she need not fear that you will not sing to her again, need she, Mr. Wyatt? Ah! I see you have brought your banjo with you this morning. That promises well."

"Miss Carr-Wynstede said last night she would like to learn to play the banjo," said Wyatt, " and I told her I should be honored if she would let me teach her."

" Have you heard from Kirkland, Margaret? " asked Ralph.

"Yes; I had a telegram just now. He is coming by the afternoon train."

" Good! " said Ralph; " and must he have a story in his pocket too? You surely cannot expect that from a Professor of Ethics at Harvard University."

"No; he need tell no story. He and Miss Carr-Wynstede are exempt from the general doom. By the bye, it is your turn to-night,

A Week away from Time. 81

Tom. I have arranged you all in my own mind, and discussion is useless. So don't lose Tom overboard this morning, Mr. Wyatt. We shall need him later."

"There is a calmness about you, Margaret, worthy of a better cause," said her brother-in-law, laughing; and the three men went down to the landing, and in a few moments were on board the "Hope," and she was under sail and off out of the Harbor, and soon out of sight, with a fair wind and all sails set, heading for Vineyard Sound. Miss Carr-Wynstede came downstairs looking very handsome and serene, followed by Marie.

"I am ready for a walk or drive, or what you will, dear Mrs. Temple," said she, "as soon as I have found out what Marie means. She tells me your maid Susan has asked her to go 'upon the sea' with her and some one whose name she cannot remember; but she says it is a name from the Holy Scriptures, and she calls him 'l'homme aux homards.' I dare say it is quite right, but I wanted to ask you."

Margaret laughed heartily. "It must mean that Jim Canaan has asked them to go out to his lobster-pots, as a delicate attention to the foreigner. Yes, it is all right. Jim is the best fellow that ever lived, though reputed a lady-killer in the neighborhood, I believe, — so let Marie beware, — and Susan goes with them for propriety's sake, and all is well. Good-by, Bell. Don't go to sleep, but weave us a romance out of the stuff this golden day is made of."

As Margaret stooped to kiss her sister, who was lying placidly in the hammock, Bell said, —

"Good-by, sister mine. How young you look to-day, and how happy! Is this the influence of the Gulf Stream that you and Ralph talk about? Blessed Gulf Stream, if it be!"

A mesure qu'on a plus d'esprit on trouve qu'il-y-a plus d'hommes originaux. Les gens de commun ne trouvent pas de différence entre les hommes.
PASCAL.

Homo sum ; humani nihil a me alienum puto.
TERENCE.

SECOND DAY.

(Continued.)

PROFESSOR KIRKLAND had telegraphed that he would walk from the station to Fair Harbor, so Ralph went to meet him that afternoon. When the two gentlemen reached the White House, they found the others sitting about under the lindens, — Bell in the hammock, covered with a yellow chuddah shawl, from the folds of which the soft black eyes of her King Charles looked sleepily forth; Margaret winding wool for her knitting, while Tom Bowdoin held the skein, and Erin lay at her feet on a very becoming rug; at a little distance, the English girl and Charlie Wyatt, the latter giving a lesson on the banjo, which they both appeared to find very absorbing. Margaret greeted the Professor cordially, as an old friend, and (such born actors are women, the simplest and honestest of them) no one would have noticed a deeper color in her cheek, or a shade more of feeling in her voice than usual, unless it may have been Kirkland himself; and he was too much taken up in trying to hide his own emotion to be a keen observer of Margaret's manner.

"I am just as glad to see you as if I got out of the hammock to greet you," said Mrs. Bowdoin. "Don't, please, expect me to do that; I am too comfortable here. Besides, no woman likes to do what she is not sure of doing gracefully; and getting out of a hammock is a crucial test."

"It would be a pity if you moved," said the Professor; "you are in perfect harmony with the scene. I supposed Mrs. Temple had arranged you as part of the 'décor.' You match the soft dreamy atmosphere, and the purple haze over the headlands, and the murmur in the pine-trees, and the summer sea yonder; in fact, you are the embodiment of Fair Harbor in its most attractive form."

"Hear, hear!" screamed Polly from her cage; and Mr. Bowdoin said, —

"I did n't know you 'd ever been here before, Philip! How well you know the shibboleth!"

"Yes; once, a long time ago," was the reply. "I was at Mattapoisett, and sailed over to call on Mrs. Temple. I have not forgotten it."

"Margaret," said her brother, "who are the people that have built the rather pretty house over there, farther toward the mouth of the Harbor? It was not there last year."

"They are Philadelphians," answered Margaret.

"'Philadelphians'!" repeated Ralph, in an indescribable tone of voice.

"You would be known for a Bostonian, just from the way you said that one word," remarked Bowdoin.

"What's the matter with Philadelphians?" asked Muriel. "Aren't they nice?"

"They are not precisely nasty, which is the English alternative, I believe," said Ralph laughing; "but they're so very, so very — Philadelphian! They have a language of their own, and they insist upon talking it before persons who are not used to it. They even defend it, and say it is correct; or else they are unconscious of it, which is more exasperating still."

"Do they really speak a separate language?" asked Muriel, looking very puzzled and serious.

"It is not exactly a language. It's a dialect; which should not astonish you, Miss Carr-Wynstede, coming from the land of dialects. I'll tell you what I mean. They have a queer way of behaving with their vowels. They eliminate the broad *a* from their speech almost entirely. They say *paaas* and *graaas* and *paaath*. They call chicken, *chickn*, and Ellen, *Elln*, and brown, *brayown*, and bird, and girl — no! you must hear a Philadelphian 'pur sang' pronounce those words; I could not do justice to them. I am speaking now of the genuine article; I do not refer to the travelled Philadelphian who has adopted the speech of other places."

"Of Boston, perhaps you would say," suggested Mr. Bowdoin. "Any one would think we had some standard by the River Charles, like the French Academy, for example."

"When I was at Newport once, before I was married," said Mrs. Bowdoin, "there was a Philadelphian quite devoted to me, who was by way of being a poet."

"Their poets are most of them 'by way of being,'" interposed Ralph. "Do you mean old Nugent, who offered himself to you in rhyme? You showed me his note. It began: —

> 'If you'll be mine,
> As I am thine,
> No ill of Time
> Can cause repine.
> Then, Bella dear—'"

"Oh, stop, Ralph, for pity's sake!" said his sister blushing. "I don't believe I ever showed you the note at all. You must have looked over my shoulder while I was answering it."

"Which you did, in prose," said Ralph.

"As I was saying before I was interrupted," continued Bell, "this gentleman invited me one day to go to walk with him on the cliffs, and as we walked he asked if he might repeat a little poem (he called it *poum*) which he had written. I begged him to do so. It began —

> 'Angel faces haaant mee pillah—'

This is all I can remember, for I was trying so hard not to laugh at the first line, I could not listen to the rest."

"There are mighty nice people among them, in spite of their *patois*," said Ralph condescendingly; "but I wish they had not discovered Fair Harbor. There are so many other places! We have had this one to ourselves for so long! Now, there is that big boarding-house across the Harbor — hotel, I believe they call it. Just fancy, a hotel at Fair Harbor! Margaret bears it so amiably, I am provoked with her."

"I bear it amiably, because I don't object to it," said Margaret. "In fact, I like it. In the first place, I am predisposed in favor of people who have the good taste to select Fair Harbor for their play-days. They must see its beauties and care for them for their own sake; and I always feel that there must be something very nice in people who love Nature and a country life *per se*."

"That theory has its dangers," remarked Mr. Bowdoin. "All persons with innocent tastes are not innocuous. We have heard that a celebrated murderer of our time cared specially for music, flowers, and little children."

"Then, besides," went on Margaret, "I like people. People, as people, as human beings, are intensely interesting to me. I have always felt that the Roman gentleman who made the celebrated remark announcing his affinity with all mankind (was it Plautus or Terence who put it into his mouth?) was my twin in sentiment."

"Yes, Margaret is quite capable of making dear friends of those Philadelphians, and of having them over here constantly," sighed Ralph; "and even, I believe, she would go so far as to row across the harbor to the hotel and make acquaintance with a lot of uninteresting people and offer them the freedom of the White House."

"How do we know they are uninteresting?" exclaimed Margaret. "How do we dare take that for granted? They may be saying the same thing of us at this moment, and we know very well how delightful we are."

"Do you mean that the majority of human beings are interesting, Mrs. Temple?" asked Wyatt; "because there I should quite disagree with you. The masses are bores. It is Matthew

Arnold's 'remnant' which saves. Elimination is tedious, but necessary. The processes are many, the expense often ruinous, before the true ore emerges, pure and shining. More than most of the time, is the game worth the candle?"

"I do not like your simile," answered Margaret. "It does not apply, if you will pardon my saying so. Human nature does not hide itself. One need not dig, or dive, or struggle for it. Here it is, in the world with us, like the sun or rain, or the air we breathe. And what do you mean by 'the masses'? Are they not composed of individuals, men and women and children, — above all, of children? So I have heard people speak of 'the poor,' and how to deal with them. As if the poor were a conglomerate lump of misfortune and ignorance, one great army of 'Les Misérables,' to be handled *en gros* and not *en détail!* Suppose doctors treated 'the sick' like that, and gave us all the same pills and powders when we were ill! It would be about as rational as your way of looking at the masses."

"I believe, truly, that Margaret delights in common people," said Mrs. Bowdoin. "That's one reason she likes horse-cars."

"Yes, I own it, Bell. I never go in the railway train from Boston to Brookline, or in a horse-car from the West End to the South End, without getting interested in some face I see or some conversation I hear. I remember I went far out of my way once, I became so absorbed in a woman and her little boy whom she was taking to the Children's Hospital. We got to be great friends afterwards,—that little boy and I. I dare say you all think me terribly democratic; but if one is too exclusive in this world, one may end by shutting out the sun."

"I cannot express how entirely I am on Mrs. Temple's side of the question," said the Professor, who had been listening attentively, and now joined in the talk. "People are altogether the most interesting things in this most interesting world. This would seem to be a self-evident proposition; but it is not, or we should not be discussing it. Every time a child is born, what possibilities it stands for! Here may be the king a nation is awaiting, the great inventor, the great philanthropist, the great poet, the great preacher, — the saviour, in some sort, of his day and generation. One thrills at the tidings, — a child is born. It is as when a city rises out of an uninhabited region; one says to one's self, here may be the cradle of a new and higher civilization!"

"Yes," said Bowdoin, "and as a general thing the child grows up to fall into line with the average mortal, — to be as commonplace, as unremunerative, as ordinary, as were his parents before him. So the new city, — its architecture as dreary, as uniform, as in the next town; its laws as mechanical and lifeless; its civilization as unprogressive. History repeats itself in individuals, in families, in nations. Archimedes' lever would be of little use in a treadmill."

"For shame! for shame!" cried Margaret. "*E pur si muove!* I thank Heaven that every day's sun shines on a new-created world. As for me, the very word 'stranger' always makes my heart beat a little quicker. When I was a young girl in society, and one said, 'Let me present Mr. So-and-so to you,' I always began by thinking, ' This may be the prince I have been dreaming of. Let me wake and try to recognize him.' "

" How often you must have been disappointed, dear Mrs. Temple," said Wyatt, "when you were thoroughly awake."

" Yes, but it never prevented my dreaming again. The prince is always somewhere in the world. One finds the world more beautiful because he is in it, even if he has never quite reached one's castle gate. Meantime the world itself is full and running over with all that makes life worth living. And why? Because in it are hundreds of millions of God's creatures with that thing we call a soul in their bodies."

" Surely there can be no lack of reasons for finding our fellow-beings interesting," added the Professor, "since to all of them come sorrow and sin and death."

There was a pause after these last words, and presently a voice was heard, saying, " Well, well! here you all are! I am so glad, now, I chose Fair Harbor!" And the owner of the voice came panting into the midst of the group, having apparently climbed the steepest part of the bank, from the water.

"Why Caroline Chauncey, my dear Caroline! where in the name of all that's welcome did you come from?" exclaimed Margaret; and Polly, who was always greatly excited over a new arrival, shouted, "Tè! Tè! Ques aco? Ques aqui?"[1] Being a Provençal parrot, she had preserved some of her native dialect. "And why did n't you let me know you were in the neighborhood?"

"For the best of reasons, my dear! I did n't know it myself till a few moments ago. You see, I meant to go to Newport for a week; and although I had invitations to my friends' houses, I refused them all, and thought I would just go to Munschinger's by myself. When I got down to the Old Colony railroad station, it suddenly occurred to me how stupid it was to go to Newport where I knew every one, and how nice it would be to go to some place I never heard of. So I went and stood by the

[1] Tiens! Tiens! Qu'est-ce-qu'il y-a? Qui est-ce?

A Week away from Time. 97

ticket-office and listened to the names of the places; and presently somebody said, 'Give me a ticket for Fair Harbor;' and I said to myself, 'What a pretty name! That's where I will go.' So I got a ticket, and when the train stopped I got out, and went up to a vehicle and asked the boy to drive me somewhere, and he said would I go to the Fair Harbor House? That seemed a practical thing to do. He took me to the house over yonder, and I said to the landlady, 'Who lives in the big white house across the river, — or is it a river?' and she said, 'Mrs. Temple.' So I told her to have me taken directly there, that I might see if it was *my* Mrs. Temple. I was put, just as I was, into a boat and rowed across; and here you are, and here am I! Do you know I like the look of things immensely, and think I shall stay a week, — especially since I have found you all."

"Then come in and dine with us," said Margaret; "that will be delightful."

"If you will let me dine in my travelling-dress. I find I have not my trunk with me. It must have been left in Boston at the station, or perhaps it went to Newport. Would you just telegraph for it, Mr. Travers," turning to Ralph, — " to both places, please? If it is not at either of them, or at my own house, I am sure I don't know where it can possibly be."

*Honest love, honest sorrow,
Honest work for the day, honest hope for the morrow,
Are these worth nothing more than the hands they make weary,
The hearts they have saddened, the lives they leave dreary?*

OWEN MEREDITH.

Ce qui importe dans le sacrifice, c'est le sacrifice même. Si l'objet pour lequel on se dévoue est une illusion, le dévouement n'en est pas moins une réalité; et cette réalité est la plus splendide parure dont l'homme puisse décorer la misère morale.

ANATOLE FRANCE.

EVENING OF SECOND DAY.

AFTER dinner, which was a very gay one, — Mrs. Chauncey's funny mistakes and inconsequences making much merriment, in which that dear lady freely joined, — Mrs. Temple said, —

"Now, Tom, what have you got for us? Something very nice, I know."

"My dear Margaret," said Bowdoin, looking a little uneasy, "I have forborne my confession until this supreme moment. I dare say you will be very angry, and perhaps refuse my contribution altogether. But what will you? Can a man who has never written an original line in his life, all of a sudden produce a story on command, even on your command, O Queen? No, of course he cannot. Yet Bell said if I did n't bring something, I could not come at all. So I searched among my papers, thinking that perhaps I might some day have written a story without knowing it; and I found—"

"Well, what did you find?" eagerly asked Margaret.

"I found this," said Tom, taking a manuscript from his pocket. "It is — now, don't frown, Margaret — it is a translation, or rather an adaptation of a story of Guy de Maupassant's. I found it in a collection of short stories last winter, and liked it so much that I translated it for my own amusement. If it is quite against your ideas to allow anything second-hand to come inside this sacred circle, I will not read it. But it is all I have."

"What does the company say?" asked the hostess, turning to the others. "Shall we have Tom's translation? My only objection would be that it might be taken as a precedent. But I believe we are pretty safe for the rest of the week, are we not?"

It was voted, with no contrary minds, that the translation should be heard; and Bowdoin read

THE STORY OF THE NECKLACE.

MONSIEUR ALPHONSE LOISEL was a clerk in what in Washington would be called the State Department. He was a faithful and painstaking official, and as he did not draw his salary from the United States Treasury, he did not live under the imminent possibility of being turned out of his position at any moment to make room for some fellow whom a member of Congress, to pay off an old political debt, wanted to put in his place. The machinery of the administration moved all the more smoothly for the care and politeness with which he attended to his part of it. He had a salary of five thousand francs, and looked forward to the continuance of it so long as he performed faithfully and well his allotted task, and could hope for a pension if in the course of time he were used up in the service of his country.

Madame Loisel was a charming young woman of twenty-five years. She was the daughter of a small tradesman who had died a year or two before her marriage, leaving her a few thousand francs. Besides having a lovely figure, she was graceful in her manners and carriage, and therefore most attractive on first acquaintance. She was a brunette, with delicate features, large, soft, dark eyes, with long lashes. She had beautiful arms and shoulders and bust, with small hands and feet. With all this, there was an air of refinement about her more attractive than her beauty. She was one of the women who seem created by Nature to be admired of men. She would have enjoyed and contributed more to what is called "society" than most of her sex, if she had had the means to do so; as it was, she had to be content with admiring the luxury of others, — in studying the brilliant toilettes which she saw in the public promenades, or at the theatres, where she went occasionally with her husband to indulge in the artificial emotions of the drama.

The most memorable day of her life had been when she went to a ball given by one of the heads of the department in which her husband was employed. That was two years before our story opens. How much she would have enjoyed one of those grand ministerial balls to which the great people from all parts of the world were glad to go! She had heard of them, and pictured to herself halls hung with cloth of gold and Gobelin tapestry; the panels and ceilings painted by celebrated artists; marble staircases lined with exotic plants which filled the air with tropical odors; mirrors reaching from floor to ceiling, and

The Story of the Necklace. 105

chandeliers of crystal brilliant with the light of innumerable candles. One day, on coming home at the usual hour, Monsieur Loisel informed his wife that it was said that in the following month one of those grand ministerial balls was about to take place. For some reason, he did not know why, it was to be exceptionally fine, — more so than any previous one. After a fortnight the rumor became a certainty, and later it was known that invitations were being sent out; but it was going to be so magnificent and select that it was very difficult, even for high officials, to procure one. There was a great stir about it. It was said that the Shah of Persia was to be there in a uniform shining like the sun with precious stones.

"How splendid it will be!" said Madame Loisel with a sigh.

"Yes, my dear," said her husband. "I have heard that the Shah has an emerald on his fez as big as a robin's egg, into which are stuck three golden feathers of some bird unknown to science."

Every day on his return home Monsieur Loisel had something new to tell his wife about the approaching ball. Once, it was that the Russian Grand-Duke was to be there with a suite of twenty-five officers; again, there were to be members of ten of the royal families of Europe. The Chinese ambassador, who had just arrived in France, was going with his suite. It was said they would all be dressed in yellow silk, which was the imperial color, and their shoes and caps, and even their underclothes, would be of the same hue, and of the finest Chinese crape. There was to be a celebrated Turkish grandee, — a general of great renown who had burned an entire village, and who had received the Albert medal from Queen Victoria, all set round with diamonds; he was to take the wife of the English ambassador in to supper. There would be Scotch officers, who generally go about with bare legs, but on this occasion they were to wear silk tights. Some Bashi-Basouks from Central Asia were going in uniforms made of camel's hair wrought with gold. The ladies would be more superbly dressed than they had ever been before. The principal jewellers of Paris had already sold half of their most precious ornaments.

"How perfectly magnificent it will be!" said Madame Loisel. "It will be like one of the Arabian Nights' tales."

Two days later Monsieur Loisel came home a quarter of an hour earlier than usual. He ran up to the third story where his apartment was, opened his door, and stood panting for breath before his astonished wife, with one hand in his breast. "My dear, what do you think I have in my pocket-book?"

"Why," she answered, "how should I know? You are all out of breath. Why did you run so? I do not know what you have. Is it seats at the opera?"

"Better than that."

"Better than that! What can it be?"

"Here," said Monsieur Loisel, taking an envelope out of his breast-pocket and offering it to her, — "here are two tickets, for you and for me, for the — for the — can you guess? — for the grand ball given by the Minister of the Interior three weeks from to-day."

"How extraordinary! Is it possible? How did you get them?" exclaimed Madame Loisel, utterly overcome at what she heard, and uncertain if she had understood aright.

"My friend Goaillet gave them to me. He could not use them himself, on account of a death in the family."

Madame Loisel took the tickets in her hand and looked at them, first on one side and then on the other. There was no mistake. There was the printed invitation, with the names written in ink. She beamed with delight. "How enchanting!" she exclaimed. "I can scarcely believe it."

After a moment, as soon as she had recovered from her first surprise, while still looking at the invitation, she turned quickly to her husband, as if a sudden and painful thought had come to her.

"My dear," she said, "what shall I wear?"

"Why," he replied, "put on the dress you go to the opera in."

"That will not do. It is not made for a ball-dress. It is not a proper one for the occasion."

"Can you not alter it so that it will do?"

"Alter it! No. It could never be made fit. How dull men are about such things! I should have to get a new dress," she added, after a pause.

This was a serious consideration. But the grand ball was such an exceptional occasion; it would be the great social event of her life; it might never occur again; she would probably never again have such a chance. It was decided that she should have a new dress. It was, however, not to cost over three hundred and fifty francs, and was to be made of some material and color that might be utilized afterward.

Madame Loisel was beside herself with joy. She immediately set about her dress. She chose a handsome yellow silk, of good quality and becoming shade. It was made décolleté, with a long train, and trimmed with lace. She worked at it herself with the dressmaker during the day, and dreamed of it at night. It

The Story of the Necklace. 109

was a great success. The fit was perfect. It became her wonderfully. She looked distinguished and beautiful in it. There was only one thing wanting to make it perfect, and that was some jewelry rich enough to complete the whole.

Madame Loisel felt this keenly; but what could be done? She had one handsome diamond ring, but that would not be an ornament for her dress. Suddenly the thought struck her that one of her old school friends, who had married a man of property, and was living in style in another part of Paris, had a good deal of jewelry, and might be willing to lend her some. Her name was Caroline Forestier. She had been one of her most intimate friends at school. Marriage had separated them somewhat, as often happens in such cases, but she had kept up a greater intimacy with her than with most of the friends of her school-days. They did not meet very often, it is true, but it was always with affection when they did.

Madame Loisel resolved to go to see her friend and ask her to lend her some of her ornaments. "My dear Caroline," said she, after the first greetings were over, "I am going day after to-morrow to the grand ball given by the Minister of the Interior." And she told her all she knew about it; how she had had an expensive dress made for the occasion, how beautiful it was, and how the only thing needed to make it perfect was some jewelry; and she ended by asking her friend to lend her some.

"My dear," said Madame Forestier, "how lovely you will look! Yellow is so becoming to you! I wish I were going to the ball, but I am not invited. I have heard that it is going to be very splendid. I will lend you some jewels with pleasure. What will you have? You may choose what you think will look best."

And thereupon she led her friend to a small safe let into the wall, and opening it with a key she wore on her watch-chain, begged her to choose. There was a necklace of gold, set with emeralds; there was another of pearls; diamond brooches, beautiful Venetian chains and bracelets. Madame Loisel looked at them one after the other; a selection was difficult; she could not make up her mind. As she was hesitating, she spied in a corner a box of light-blue velvet which had not been opened. She drew it toward her. It contained a rivière of diamonds.

"Oh, how magnificent!" she exclaimed. "But I dare not ask you for that. It is too precious to lend."

"You may, my dear," answered her friend. "Why not? You may take it if you desire to so much."

Madame Loisel fell on Caroline's neck and embraced her. When she left, she carried home the treasure with her.

The appointed evening came. Madame Loisel was at the great ball. As soon as she arrived she attracted as much attention as any one there. She was very handsome, and it was a new face. Two ladies of great fashion, after surveying her carefully from head to foot, though they had to admit that she was very striking-looking, came to the conclusion that the richness of her dress did not correspond to that of her necklace.

"I wonder where she got that necklace?" said one to the other. "Do you know who she is?"

"No, my dear; I never saw her before. She must be a stranger. I thought she came in with an American-looking man."

"But if she were an American, her dress would be extravagantly rich; even too much so. Hers is too simple for the necklace, and it is not studied simplicity either."

The men, however, made up by their attentions for any disparaging remarks of the other sex. They vied with each other to be presented to her. Officers, who were as satisfied with their uniforms as Madame Loisel was with her dress, crowded round her, those with higher titles, or of higher rank, gently pushing the inferior ones aside. Diplomats, noblemen, distinguished authors, men of science, gazed at her as she passed. An English earl was so charmed with her that he spoke English to her for ten minutes before finding out that she did not understand a word of it; and he had to give way to a German duke who had thirty orders on his breast. A successful American speculator was so much pleased with her that he invited her and her husband to come and visit him at Chicago, saying that he would pay all their travelling expenses. After much skirmishing with an Italian prince, who was also a grandee of Spain, one of the financial powers of London succeeded in leading her in to supper, and besought her to be present at a ball that was to be given in a month at the English Embassy, saying that H. R. H. the Prince of Wales, would probably be there, and asking for the honor of sending her as many invitations as she desired. The Russian Grand-Duke was presented to her, and ordered his aide-de-camp to see that she was invited to the Russian Embassy. It was the happiest evening of her life. She was courted and admired and flattered, and pleased with herself, and Monsieur Loisel was sincerely proud of his beautiful wife.

But every joy must come to an end. Toward four o'clock in the morning the salons were being deserted.

The Story of the Necklace. 113

Madame Loisel had stayed almost to the last. Her husband had been patiently waiting for her, quietly dozing on a chair, in one of the side-rooms, with several other men doing the same thing while waiting for their wives. Monsieur Loisel threw over his wife's shoulders a cloak which contrasted strongly by its simplicity with her dress, and with the rich wraps and furs that the ladies put on who were leaving at the same time; and they hurried off, down the grand staircase, between the double rows of liveried servants, and past the gorgeous sentinels on guard at the entrance. There was no cab to be seen. They walked down the street looking about for some means of getting home. At last, in a remote corner, they found an old tumble-down cab, the horse of which was asleep in the shafts, and the owner asleep on the box. They woke the man; he started up his horse, and they drove home. It was half-past five in the morning. Monsieur Loisel was tired and sleepy, as he went upstairs to their apartment, knowing that he would have to be at his desk at nine o'clock. His wife was too much excited to feel fatigued. She had had such a bewildering night — and there was to be another ball next month at the English Embassy. She took off her cloak in front of the looking-glass in the parlor to have one more farewell look at herself in her ball-dress. Suddenly she turned pale, put her hand up to her neck, staggered for a second, uttered a cry, and remained motionless as a statue, with her eyes wide open, staring at herself in the mirror.

"What is the matter?" said her husband, coming from the bedroom.

"I have lost the necklace!" exclaimed his wife.

Monsieur Loisel turned pale in his turn. "You have lost Madame Forestier's necklace?"

"Yes, I have!" gasped the unhappy woman.

They began searching for it — in her cloak, in the folds of her dress — everywhere; but it was not to be found.

"Are you sure you had it when you left the ball-room?"

"Yes, I put my hand up to feel for it the last thing I did before leaving the house."

"Do you think you could have left it in the carriage?"

"Do I know! I must have dropped it in the street. I know I had it on when I left the palace."

Monsieur Loisel put on his coat and hurried out, jumped into a cab and drove to the door of the palace by which they had left after the ball. He then followed on foot the street they had taken in coming home an hour before. He searched the steps of the palace, the gutters, the doorways, — everywhere; he found nothing. He went to the police office to state the loss, to the overseers of the pawn-shops, to the officers of the cab companies. He advertised the necklace, promising a large reward to the finder who should return it, and no questions asked. In the afternoon he returned home : his wife had passed the day in a worse state of mind than he. After a week they gave up all hope of finding the necklace. They both looked ten years older.

"We must get a necklace just like it for Madame Forestier," said the husband.

They took the box to the jeweller whose name was printed in the inside. He looked at it, consulted his books, and said, "'The box is mine, but I did not sell the necklace you describe. I have none similar to it." They went from jeweller to jeweller, trying to find something sufficiently like the lost ornament to put in its place. At last they found one which Madame Loisel thought almost exactly like it. The price was 40,000 francs. The jeweller promised to keep it for them for three days, and to take it back for 35,000 francs any time within three months, in case the other necklace should turn up.

Monsieur Loisel and his wife did not possess anything approaching the sum needed. They took all they had — carried all they could to the pawnbroker's, asked one friend to loan them 2,000 francs, one or two 500, or what they could spare; they borrowed the rest from money-lenders at thirty to forty per cent interest; and at the end of another week, with bankruptcy and poverty staring them in the face, Monsieur Loisel went to the jeweller, paid him 40,000 francs, and received the necklace. The next day Madame Loisel carried it to her friend.

"I thought you would have returned it sooner. I might have wanted it to wear myself," said Madame Forestier, who evidently had not seen the advertisements in the newspapers. She put the box back in the safe as she spoke. Then, turning to her friend, she said, —

"But you promised to tell me about the ball. How did you enjoy it?"

"Oh, I cannot tell you now!" said Madame Loisel; and bidding her friend a hurried good-by, she went home.

Now came for the Loisels a life of poverty. They sent off their "bonne;" they gave up their apartment, and took a few rooms in one of the poor quarters of the city, way upstairs in a narrow, dirty street. Madame Loisel had to do all the work of the household, the cooking as well as the washing. She dried her clothes on a line running from her window to a hook in the

The Story of the Necklace. 117

wall on the opposite side of the yard. They had to bring up the water from the street, and carry down the ashes. Dressed in an old stained gown, with holes in her shoes, and well-darned stockings, Madame Loisel wandered out to get food where it was cheapest, and buy the adulterated groceries with which the poor have to be satisfied. She often went hungry, that her husband might have something to eat when he came home in the evening. Every month Monsieur Loisel had to pay the interest on his notes, and was often glad to renew them at the same exorbitant rates. He passed part of his nights in copying manuscripts at five sous a page, while in the evenings he kept the books of a small shopkeeper in the neighborhood. Sometimes in the afternoon Madame Loisel would sit at the window looking on the street before her husband had returned from his office, and after she had finished the hard work of the day, and think of that happiest evening of her life, and of all the misery that had come of it.

This life lasted ten years. One evening Monsieur Loisel came home with a piece of paper in his hand, and laying it on the table, said, " At last ! This is the last bill we owe ! Everything is paid." But he and his wife had become old people. She was stout and coarse and wrinkled.

One Sunday, not long after Monsieur Loisel had paid up the capital of his debts and their compound interest, Madame Loisel strolled out into the Champs Elysées to get a little rest and fresh air after the work and confinement of the week. She was suddenly attracted by the appearance of a lady who was walking with a child not far off. She looked at her long and steadily, and thought she recognized her former friend, Caroline Forestier, whom she had not seen since the day she returned the diamond necklace, ten years ago. She was still young and handsome, while Madame Loisel felt that she herself was worn and wrinkled and dilapidated. "I must speak to her," she said to herself. "Now we have paid up everything, I can tell her the story and not be ashamed." And going up to her, she said, "Good-morning, Caroline!" The lady looked up, surprised at being greeted so familiarly by so common-looking a person whom she did not know, and said, —

"You have made a mistake, I believe."

"Pardon me, I think not. Are you not Caroline Forestier?"

"Yes, that is my name, but I do not remember ever having seen you before."

"Caroline, I am Mathilde Loisel."

"You Mathilde Loisel!" exclaimed Madame Forestier, recalling the memories of former days. "Where do you come from? How changed you are! I tried long ago to find you at your former lodgings, but you had gone away, and left no address. I did not know you."

"Since I saw you last," said Madame Loisel, "we have had — my husband and I — a hard life, and you had something to do with it."

"I!" repeated Madame Forestier. "I had something to do with your life!"

"Yes, yes; you! Do you remember lending me your diamond necklace, ten years ago, to go to the ball given at the Ministerial Palace?"

"Yes, surely; but what had that to do —"

"I lost it the night I wore it."

"You lost it! But you brought it back to me a fortnight afterward. I remember it very well, for it was the last time I ever saw you."

"No, I did not bring it back to you. I brought you another one, like it. It cost 40,000 francs. My husband and I have been working and economizing ever since to pay for it; and we have done it at last. I am not ashamed to tell you the truth. When I brought the necklace to you, you put it away without even looking at it."

"Do you mean to say that you paid 40,000 francs for the necklace you brought me for the one I lent you?"

"Yes, we did; and it has taken us ten years."

Madame Forestier looked at her old friend hardly able to speak, and then taking both her hands she said, "Mathilde, my necklace was not of diamonds: it was of paste. The whole thing was not worth 500 francs."

"It is a very nice story," said Mrs. Chauncey, — "very nice; only it was too bad that she should have grown so old and plain. It seems so strange, too, in Paris, where they have all sorts of cosmetics and things. Why, I met Mrs. Wiggin in Beacon Street the other day. She has been living in Paris for five years, you know. She's sixty if she's a day; and what with her golden blond hair and her Worth clothes, she looks twenty-five."

"You will sing to us to-night, Muriel, will you not?" said Mrs. Temple.

"Yes, willingly," replied Muriel, going to the piano. She ran over the keys for a few moments, preluding dreamily; and Margaret saw that she was really musical, which is not necessarily the case with every one who plays and sings. Presently she struck a few chords, and sang: —

"In the summer twilight,
 While yet the dew was hoar,
I went plucking purple pansies,
 Till my love should come to shore.
The fishing-lights their dances
 Were keeping out at sea,
And 'Come,' I sang, 'my true love,
 Come, hasten home to me!'

"But the sea it fell a-moaning,
 And the white gulls rocked thereon,
And the young moon dropped from heaven,
 And the lights hid one by one.
And silently their glances
 Slipped down the cruel sea,
And 'Wait,' cried the night-wind and the storm,
 'Wait till I come to thee.'"[1]

Charlie Wyatt had been gazing with a rapt, adoring expression at Miss Carr-Wynstede while she sang, and with the utter unconsciousness that any one might be observing him, which betokens a man very far gone indeed. He went toward her when the song was finished.

"I never heard those words set to music," he said. "They are great favorites of mine."

"Will you sing the song you were speaking to me of this morning?" asked Muriel.

[1] The words by Mrs. Harriet Prescott Spofford.

Wyatt took the guitar and sang: —

"Thy claim alone I wait,
If soon or late it summon me —
　Stranded like yon imprisoned boat,
　Till the compelling tide shall lift or float,
And bear out unresisting to the longed-for sea,
So will I wait that one full hour with thee!

"No other love than thine;
Though the slow hours ebb wearily,
　False voices tempt from off the shore,
　One song once-sung I hear forever more,
One light burns clear and white across the blackest sea;
One hour the flood-tide of thy love shall set me free."

Afterward Muriel and Wyatt sang together Italian, German, English songs. Muriel's voice was a mezzo-soprano, with deep, tender, low notes, and the two voices blended perfectly together.

"Confound the fellow!" whispered Ralph to his brother-in-law; "isn't it enough that he should be as handsome as that, without singing love-songs in a way that no woman can be expected to resist, into the bargain?"

"It is a little rough on the rest of us," said Bowdoin laughing; and to himself he thought, "Oho, Mr. Ralph! sits the wind in that quarter?"

And when she was embarked, did you not mark how the waves whistled, and the seas danced for joy, and all because they had Urania.
                    SIR PHILIP SIDNEY'S *Arcadia.*

The great sweet mother, mother and lover of men, the sea!
                                        SWINBURNE.

THIRD DAY.

It was in very truth a perfect day, the one they had chosen for sailing to Waquoit. Even Mrs. Bowdoin was tempted from the hammock, — to her own great surprise, — and found herself on board the "Hope" at ten o'clock in the morning, with the rest of the party, Mrs. Chauncey included, who had brought a life-preserver with her from the hotel, but had been induced by Mrs. Temple to leave it behind, as it might hurt Mr. Wyatt's feelings. To judge by the rapturous expression on that handsome face, nothing could ruffle him to-day, or mar the absolute joy he felt that Muriel's feet were at last treading the deck of his vessel. He blushed all to himself that he could ever have said what he did (and now remembered with an agony of shame) to Mrs. Bowdoin. "What an idiot I was!" he muttered. This was to be an all-day expedition, and they were to lunch on board. Margaret had consulted with Captain Nye, and had found that they were picking cranberries at Waquoit,— a function she especially wanted the English girl to witness, as being something the like of which she had never seen, and could see nowhere else so well.

"I have sent horses and traps to meet us at Waquoit Bay," said Mrs. Temple. "They will take us to the cranberry bog I think best worth seeing, and if any of you prefer land-travel to a sea-voyage, they shall be at your disposition to bring you home."

"As the wind is fair, and as we have the day before us," said Wyatt, "I thought we would go round Naushon into Vineyard Sound. When we come back, if the tide serves, we will make the short-cut through the Holl, by Nobska-light."

"How charming those names are!" said Muriel. "Whenever I hear the Indian names in this country, I wonder that I hear them so seldom. And I dare say they all mean something. Waquoit, for instance?"

"They say it came from the call of the quail," answered Wyatt; "and certainly it is as much like it as 'More wet! More wet!' which is unreliable meteorologically, or 'Bob White!' which is prosaic and unmeaning. See! is not the island of Naushon pretty?"

As Wyatt spoke, they were sailing near to the shore of Naushon, by Kettle Cove, and out from the thicket came a deer, quite down to the water's edge. The beautiful creature looked at the vessel for a moment with her great, soft, startled eyes, and bounded back into the forest. A kingfisher stood on the beach, on one leg, and calmly watched the "Hope" sail by. Sheldrakes and gulls flew over their heads, and in the woods beyond, the quail were calling "Waquoit! Waquoit!" A thick growth of oaks and maples in their autumn bravery made a fringe of color quite down to the narrow line of white beach-sand, so that the brilliant hues were reflected in the water.

"How very, very beautiful it is!" said Muriel with enthusiasm. "I have never seen anything quite like it."

"There is always something very fascinating to me about an island," said Margaret. "I shall never forget one beautiful day in January, at Cannes, when I went over in a boat to the islands of Ste. Marguerite and St. Honorât. After doing what was expected of us in visiting the fortress at Ste. Marguerite, and the cell where the 'Man with the Iron Mask' was shut up, and looking at the wall over which General Bazaine escaped two centuries later, we walked across the island through a wonderful forest of stone-pines bowed by the winds, and olive-trees whose charm is too subtle and mysterious to be told on canvas or by any words, and came out to the water again. Here a boat took us across to the Isle St. Honorât. I can hardly say why this place appealed so strongly to my imagination, but truly that day I felt as I suppose poets feel every day. There is a monastery at one end of the island, — one of the oldest in France, — within whose cloistered walls live monks of a silent order. They never speak except to say their prayers; and I fancied I could hear, in the still air, the echoes of the Ave Marias and the Amens as they were chanted from cell to cell. Outside the walls of the cloister garden, into which no woman's foot ever penetrated, were alleys bordered with box and rosemary, which filled the air with sweet odors. The waves washed the stony beach at our feet, and wild flowers and tall canes and rushes grew thick on the craggy banks. I sat down in a little empty chapel looking out to sea, and wanted to stay forever. I believe I would have taken the vow of perpetual silence, if those stern, white-cowled monks would have let me in. For days and days the place haunted me; and at night, when the moon shone, I fancied it lighting up the cells and corridors of the 'Moines Silencieux,' and again I heard the echoes of the Aves and the long Amen."

"How can men make such asses of themselves?" was Ralph's slightly brusque exclamation.

"It does not seem to me so remarkable," said Tom Bowdoin. "I dare say they had heard too much talk. They had probably all been married men. Now, what does surprise me, is to learn that there is an order, somewhere, of

'Sœurs Silencieuses!' That, indeed, is phenomenal, and contrary to nature."

"I think I would rather live at Naushon," remarked Muriel.

"It's very pretty," said Mrs. Chauncey; "but one might as well be Robinson Crusoe, or a babe in the wood, and done with it. And just think, in case of fire! and evenings! No one to drop in, and no theatre or anything, and those dreadful gulls screaming. I should go crazy, I am sure!"

The yacht had rounded Naushon, and was sailing up Vineyard Sound, and to the southeast Martha's Vineyard lay misty and purple in the distance.

"Does the entire vineyard belong to Martha?" asked Mrs. Chauncey,—"and who is Martha, at any rate? I dare say you think me very ignorant, but I have heard of her all my life, and have always meant to ask some one who knew. Can't we go there some day?"

"Ah! never; let me beg you, never!" exclaimed Mrs. Temple. "I, too, year after year have sailed by that island, as we are sailing now, and thought how attractive it looked, veiled in mist, clad in the grace of distance. One day — one rash day — I made Ralph take me there. We landed at Oak Bluff. It was camp-meeting time. We drove to Cottage City. I spoke never a word till we were on board my boat again. Then I drew a long breath, and said, 'Oh, horrible! horrible! most horrible!' I felt like Rosamond with her purple jar. No, let me spare you that disillusion. Never tear away that veil; there are ghastly horrors behind it. 'Non ragionam di lor, ma guarda e passa!'"

"Why, with your love of the masses, I should think you'd rather like a cottage at Oak Bluff," said Bell. "It would be better than horse-cars, because more of it."

Margaret looked scornful, but made no reply. Steering northward now, they passed Menahaut, — another Indian name for Muriel, — and came into Waquoit Bay, past Monamascoy Island. She wrote the names down, and said she had a favorite cat at home, who should be christened Monamascoy as soon as she got back to Devonshire.

As the sloop came about just before going into the Bay, her sail hit Mrs. Chauncey's red parasol, which she was holding high over her head, and knocked it into the water.

"It was my fault," said Wyatt, who was at the helm (for though he had an excellent skipper, he liked sometimes to sail his own boat). "I should have warned you."

"Don't mention it," said the most good-natured of women. "I really ought to have known myself; for when poor dear Paul was alive he used to take me sailing a good deal, and I might have known that when you took in a tuck (that's what you call it, I believe) I should have put down my parasol. I really used to know a good deal about boats, Paul being an architect, you know. I knew all the sails; the mainsail (mainsle, you have to say), and boomsle, and sternsle, and all; and I used to sing, —

'Give me a wet sheet and a flowing sail.'

You all know it; though why they wanted to sleep in damp sheets, I never could think — it's so unhealthy. To make them hardy, I suppose."

It was luncheon-time when the "Hope" cast anchor in the pretty bay; and as the whole party agreed that it was a pity to go below and so lose sight of the wooded shores and curving beaches, they lunched on deck sumptuously, and Mrs. Chauncey declared that if she only shut her eyes she should imagine herself at Delmonico's. "But I will *not* shut my eyes," said she firmly, with something of a Spartan air.

On shore they found vehicles waiting for them. Mrs. Temple and the Professor led the way up through the lane leading to the little village, through the village, past the old mill, by a wood-road, out upon the cranberry bog. They left their carriages and walked a short distance, across a wooden bridge, and found themselves looking upon what was to most of them as novel a scene as it was to the English girl. The harvest of the cranberry is an important epoch to the dwellers on the south side of Cape Cod. It may be called the industry of that region, as the salting and packing of codfish is of other parts. Every autumn, before the hard frosts come, the "raccolte" of the berry takes place. The school-children are given a vacation of three or four days, and young and old devote themselves to the gathering of the fruit without which no Thanksgiving or Christmas dinner in New England is complete.

This special bog, on this special day, presented a memorable sight. A piece of cleared land of ten or twelve acres, of no great value for other purposes, had been consecrated to cranberry culture, and this year's yield was reported to be a remarkably fine one. The delicate vine, with its myrtle-green leaves, ran thick and close, close to the sandy soil; underneath, when you stooped to look, you saw the rich crimson berries, with a purple bloom on them. Indeed, when one looked over the whole wide acres, the ruddy fruit cast a warm tinge up through the green, as one sees the blood-red heart of the alexandrite glowing through the deep green of the stone.

This cranberry bog was set in a frame of bright foliage; shrub oaks, their leaves, "some stained as with blood, and made crimson, and

A Week away from Time. 135

some as with tears;" maples, scarlet and gold in the sunshine; red woodbine running riot over the trunks of old pines; all sorts of bright bushes and vines joining hands to dress the festival with the gayest they could give; and kneeling on the ground were women and children by scores, silently picking and filling the measures as if performing some sacred rite. Here and there a bright shawl on one of the women, or a gay handkerchief round a girl's neck, or a colored ribbon knotted in her braids, made a spot of sympathetic color among the crowd. One little fellow looked up as the party approached, and caught sight of Joujou in Mrs. Bowdoin's arms. "Oh, look, mother, look!" he cried; "that's the littlest dog I ever saw! Just see his tail!" The woman never raised her head. "PICK!" she shouted in stern, stentorian tones from the depths of her sunbonnet to the small boy, who hung his head and obeyed the mandate. What were little dogs or their tails, when weighed in the balance with his stint of so many quarts an hour! Each picker is provided with a tin measure into which he drops the berries as he pulls them from the vines. He is paid so much for each measure. These are poured into larger receptacles, and finally into bushel-baskets. Inspectors walk about, and take account of what each one does, and shout the tally across the fields to the head man, who marks it all down. The bushel-basketfuls are poured into sacks, which are piled upon barrows and carried off to fill the carts awaiting them by the roadside. Muriel saw one of these barrows being carried slowly along by two men, one at each end; they seemed to be singing as they walked, and their song came over the field in a sort of solemn chant.

"See!" said Muriel; "the funeral of the cranberry! Could anything be more picturesque?"

"And they are as unconscious of making pictures," said Ralph, who stood by her side, "as any of Millet's French peasants."

Margaret Temple had been walking about among the people, recognizing here and there an old acquaintance. As she passed the small boy, who now wouldn't have looked up if a cannon had been fired close to him, she stooped and put a bit of silver in his quart measure. "Now you may look at the little dog for a moment," she said; and Joujou was patted, and wagged his tail, much to the small boy's delight, and the grim maternal face relaxed into the brief semblance of a smile.

"When Paul and I were in Cuba," said Mrs. Chauncey, as they were walking back to the carriages, "we went to a coffee-picking on a plantation. It was just like this, only, of course, they were slaves, and there were slave-drivers with long whips, and the men were almost naked, and it was entirely different — still — " and they all said they knew exactly what Mrs. Chauncey meant.

The vehicles drove back to Fair Harbor empty as they had come. The "Hope" bore her precious freight proudly home, and came up to her moorings just as the sun was setting. "Thank you for the happiest day of my life," whispered Charlie Wyatt to Muriel.

> *Let's talk of graves, of worms, and epitaphs.*
> SHAKESPEARE.

> *Ah, what white thing at the door has crossed!*
> DANTE GABRIEL ROSSETTI.

> *With bodiless form and unapparent feet.*
> IBID.

*A thousand pushing weeds the borders hold,
And standing with them, wild and rank as they,
Are tender blossoms, now grown overbold,
And careless of the garden's slow decay.
Oh, far away, in some serener air,
The eyes that loved them see a heavenly dawn;
How can they bloom without her tender care?
Why should they live, when her sweet life is gone?*

*And 'gainst its walls the city's heart still beats,
And out from it each summer wind that blows,
Carries some sweetness to the tired streets.*
MARGARET DELAND.

EVENING OF THIRD DAY.

Mr. Bowdoin excused himself for being five minutes late when he came downstairs dressed for dinner. "Captain Nye and I took a walk to the old churchyard between here and Falmouth just now," he said, "and I lingered longer than I meant to, trying to decipher some inscriptions by the dim twilight."

"You told me you were making a comparative collection of New England epitaphs," said Professor Kirkland. "Do you find that the mortuary sentiment of the interior suffers any sea-change on the borders of salt water?"

"Perhaps you find these doleful compositions more vague in expression," suggested Mrs. Temple, "and, so to speak, more modern than your gleanings from our mountain towns. Perhaps it seems easier to reach heaven from the top of a hill; whereas the hazards of this present life to those who get their bread upon the treacherous deep would be likely to cast a sea-haze over that which is to come."

"Well generalized, Margaret," replied Bowdoin. "It is only a pity that a speculation so thoughtful and subtle should not accord with the fact. But the truth is that maritime populations want a more cheerful faith than those living upon our green uplands. When you look over my collection, you will find a distempered self-consciousness about the inland epitaphs which is somewhat repulsive. Their warning outcries make little impression upon a generation which thinks it knows too much to be scared so easily." He took a slip of paper from his pocket. "Let me contrast them with this verse which I copied an hour ago. The stone, as nearly as I could make it out, bore the date 1742.

> ' Beneath this sod I lie content :
> Come rest with me : but first repent :
> And when the trumpet sounds "Arise!"
> Together we will seek the skies.'

Did you ever get an invitation that was more hospitable, hearty, and matter-of-fact? Observe that the remark about repentance is not made offensively prominent. It is thrown out by the way, as one might say. 'If you come to the picnic, don't forget your umbrella.'"

"I admire the strong assertion of the 'Ego' in your verse," said Margaret. "It is no miserable matter of lime and carbon, but *I* who lie here. It is *I* who propose to enter my bourgeois mansion in the sky, and in your good company, if you will! It is a pity that this honest mariner could not have attended the theosophic conversations at Mrs. Spring's last winter. He would have learned that while John Brown's essence might go marching on, it was very doubtful whether it must carry its baggage of personality throughout the eternal tramp."

"To change the subject for a moment," said Mrs. Bowdoin, "and to leave immortality for more fleeting themes, who is to be victimized to-night? I wish to state that my story is not finished, but that I hope to lay it before an indulgent audience in a day or two, if I am left in tolerable peace to-morrow."

"Mr. Wyatt has something for us to-night, I believe," said Margaret.

Antinous blushed violently, tugged hard at his yellow moustache, and said: "I have a poor little thing at the service of you all, and shall be only too glad to read it and have it over. It has one merit. It is not long."

After dinner, and when the company were assembled in the library, Wyatt said: "My story is really very short and quite dismal. Can't we do something a little cheerful first, before I plunge you all in gloom? Miss Carr-Wynstede, cannot you suggest something?"

"While you were all talking at dinner of epitaphs and things appertaining," answered Muriel, "I was reminded of a sort of game we have sometimes played at home. Games and epitaphs do not seem to belong together, and perhaps this is not precisely what Mr. Wyatt means by something cheerful."

"Do tell us your game, and let us play it," they all exclaimed.

"You must furnish paper and pencils then, and let us sit at the big round table, dear Mrs.

A Week away from Time. 145

Temple. And in the first place, it is really no game at all. I think papa invented it one evening when we were a Christmas party in the country and had exhausted all ordinary amusements. You may find it very tiresome. It is just this: We took some well-known verse of poetry, and each one of us tried to write it down in other words, preserving the sense. Somehow epitaphs seemed to lend themselves better than other things to this trial of wits; and the reason I thought of it at dinner was because the first verse we took was Tennyson's epitaph on Sir John Franklin in Westminster Abbey."

"Let us take the very same, and see what we can do with it!" exclaimed Margaret. "I remember it begins with a ringing, 'Not here!' Let me see, how does it go on?"

"You will let me only listen, won't you?" said Muriel. "I am sure you will all be much cleverer at it than we were; and I have got what they all wrote so jumbled in my head, I could never write an original line, I am sure."

"And I am too scared at the idea of what is before me, to think of anything else," said

Wyatt; "so please count me out, too. Let me listen with Miss Carr-Wynstede." And he drew his chair near hers.

"Are not these the lines?" said the Professor,—

"'Not here! The white North hath thy bones, and thou,
    Heroic sailor-soul,
Art passing on thine happier voyage now,
    Toward no earthly pole.'"

"It is a noble stanza, is it not?" said Margaret. "It seems almost audacious to tamper with it."

"Not at all!" exclaimed Bowdoin. "Let us pull it to pieces before we attempt to put it together again. The lines are well enough, but I think an inscription addressed to the general public should be comprehensible at a glance. Now, the words 'voy-age' and 'to-ward' are so commonly pronounced as monosyllables that one boggles at them before discovering that an unusual pronunciation is wanted here. Then there is the 'passing.' Who ever speaks of 'passing' on a voyage? The idea is poetical, if you

A Week away from Time. 147

will, but it takes too much time to get at it. Sight-seers doing the Abbey are naturally in a hurry; you must hit them on the wing, or lose your shot. Now, notice the precision with which my Barnstable County rhymer hits the mark. First, we have the bold personation of his deceased friend, then that startling invitation to the passer-by, and finally the lift to the skies where the imagination is at liberty to shape things as it chooses. No; I don't say that my man's production is better poetry, but I do say that it better answers the purpose for which inscriptions are cut upon gravestones."

"I object to your objections," said the Professor. "As to the pronunciation of the two words, it is by no means unusual in poetry; and your tourist must be in a desperate hurry (Lord Tennyson might well urge that his epitaph was not intended for hurried tourists), or have a very poor ear, if he does not detect the reading directly. Your stricture upon the word 'passing' strikes me as wholly hypercritical. Put the words in prose, and see: 'Thou art passing toward no earthly pole ['as thou sailest,' understood] on thine happier voyage.' I insist that this is clear. And you make no allowance for the difficult conditions under which the poet wrote. Suppose the late Dean Stanley had applied to you for lines in verse upon Sir John Franklin, and requested you to put in the fact that he is not buried under his monument, as is usually the case in Westminster Abbey! I wonder what sort of poetry he would have got!"

"Probably no poetry at all, as I profess no gift in that direction; but he would have got something not amenable to my criticism upon what he did get," said Bowdoin decidedly.

"As, for example," said Margaret. "Come, here is a pencil, some paper, and a book to write upon."

"Keep still for a moment, and I will try," replied her brother-in-law. "Let me see — who will give me a rhyme to 'freed'? Miss Carr-Wynstede, come to the rescue, since you got us into the scrape."

"There is 'steed,'" said Muriel, "and 'reed,' 'bead,' 'indeed'—"

"'Indeed' will do. Now, then, what do you say to this? —

'Explorer of our Western Zones,
On frozen shores thy soul was freed:
While drift the snows about thy bones,
Thou sail'st on seas unknown indeed.'"

"I don't like the touch of agnosticism in the last line," said Margaret. "It seems out of place in a Christian temple."

"Your first line is vastly inferior to Tennyson's," decreed the Professor. "We miss the arresting effect of those two opening words. They are the last things one expects to see, and impressive accordingly."

"I did n't know we undertook to make lines superior, or equal to Tennyson's," said Bowdoin; "I only said I would write something which should not have the same faults I found in his. Suppose you illustrate your criticism of my effort by one of your own."

"I will do my best," replied Kirkland. "But pray all of you be patient. It may take me some time."

"Time is as abundant as sand on the Cape," said Ralph. "Take some paper, and we shall not watch the clock."

After a few moments' silence the Professor said he was ready, though he had not been able to achieve an initiatory shock which should tingle the news to his own satisfaction.

> "'Sail northward! Thou shalt find his grave,
> Without a monument or name.
> Here, honored with our Wise and Brave,
> A grateful nation guards his fame.'"

"Very good," acknowledged Bowdoin. "Still, I think you are over-confident in predicting poor Sir John's place of sepulture, with such very definite directions as to where we're to look for it: 'Turn up on your right hand at the next turning, but at the next turning of all, on your left; marry, at the next turning, turn of no hand, but turn down indirectly to the Jew's house.' Launcelot's directions to his father are, to be sure, almost as bewildering; but then, he did not commit himself to the assertion that Shylock's house would be found."

"I think myself," said Mrs. Bowdoin, "that it might be well to localize the spot more decidedly. Why not introduce some Northern flora or fauna? You lose your way too easily among those Arctic snow-drifts."

"I don't know what sort of flora you could get to grow there; and as to the fauna, remember that a single stanza does not give room to run much of a menagerie," said the Professor.

"Something in that way might be done," persisted the lady. "Wait a bit, and I will prove it. Here, now, here come my characteristic beasts:

'The white bear and the Arctic fox
Are mourners by thy Northern tomb;
England her Abbey-door unlocks,
To give thy fame its fitting room.'"

"You have brought in your fauna with a realism that makes one shiver," exclaimed Ralph. "But why, in Heaven's name, should these simple wanderers wear crape upon their left legs for the leader of an expedition that was devoted to shooting and trapping them? Come back to Shakespeare again, and get your bearings. A true poet would have perceived that those poor innocents must have regarded Sir John and his comrades as

> 'Mere usurpers, tyrants, and what 's worse,
> To fright the animals and kill them up
> In their assigned and native dwelling-place.'

Mourners by his tomb indeed! If you endow your poor beasts with human sentiments, let them at least be such as they would naturally entertain. May I amend your second line thus:—

> 'The white bear and the Arctic fox
> Dance gayly by thy Northern tomb'?"

"Ah!" said Bell, "any poetry can be killed by whipping out a carpenter's rule to take its measure. Such a miserable literalist as you are should be kept out of Westminster Abbey by act of Parliament. Of course it would be easy to meet your objection by a change which would leave dignity in the verse. If we read the line

> 'Roam scathless by thy Northern tomb,'

nobody could demur except those who had the good taste to see that it was better as I first wrote it. But come, Sir Critic, give us your version, and tell us just how the lines should have been written."

"The facts should be expressed boldly, and in the fewest possible words," said Ralph. "It should be something with a quaint, old-fashioned air, to harmonize with the surroundings. Bowdoin's last-century poet of the Falmouth churchyard would know just what to say. I will give you something in his style — well, like this, for instance, —

> 'Shrouded in snows,
> His bones repose;
> Here with the great,
> He keepeth state.'

There is the whole story at a glance. The authorities at the Abbey should be asked to adopt it. Then we should get rid of the objectionable 'voy-age' and 'to-ward,' and of the doubtful 'passing.'"

"Don't take my criticisms too seriously," said Bowdoin. "I rather meant them as part of the play. The maxim in mechanics that nothing is stronger than its weakest part, must be reversed in poetry. A strong couplet or stanza will invigorate a weak environment. Let us confess that Tennyson's first two lines are perfect. The Northern burial is petrified, as it were, in the mind of the reader, and 'heroic sailor-soul' is finely descriptive. Now, Margaret, it is your turn. Why is n't Mrs. Chauncey here this evening? She would have given us something delightful, I have no doubt."

"She sent a note just before dinner, saying that her face was so burned by her sea-voyage she was not fit to appear," said Margaret. "I am sure she would have written better lines than I can possibly evolve. She has quite a poetic vein, though it runs a little crookedly and unexpectedly." Margaret took a pencil and presently read aloud —

> "'Here, in this storied, consecrated Fane
> Thou art not laid; yet we, on bended knee,
> Thank God that, dying on the Northern main,
> Thou livest where "there shall be no more sea."'

Now," said Margaret, "I beg, no criticism of my lines; not that I could not bear it as bravely as you have all done, but because it is high time we heard Mr. Wyatt's story. Then let us agree that since none of the present company were within reach at the time, Dean Stanley did well to ask Tennyson to commemorate Sir John Franklin in Westminster Abbey! So now, dear Mr. Yachtsman, your story, if you please."

They left the table where they had been writing, and grouped themselves around the big fireplace, in which a cheerful wood-fire was blazing, in various attitudes of comfortable expectancy. Wyatt betook himself and his manuscript to a small table where was a shaded lamp, and in a sort of half-desperate, half-deprecating voice, said, —

" How I wish I too had brought a translation, as Bowdoin did, and so had braved your displeasure rather than run the risk of your contempt. When I received Mrs. Temple's delightful invitation to make one of this party, I was so bent upon acceptance, that I forgot, or thought lightly, of her command to bring a story with me. As if one kept stories in one's bureau drawers with one's pocket-handkerchiefs! As I was painfully trying to conjure up some ideas from which a story might be made, sitting in my office in Court Street, staring vacantly at my window-panes, I glanced over to the dust-thickened windows of my friend Dutton, about whose apparently colorless life I had sometimes pleased myself with weaving a vague romance, — why, I cannot say, except that the very absence of romance in his outward existence provoked me to believe that the real man carried about with him unrevealed possibilities of sentiment. So I set myself to thinking what sort of tale he would have told if he had been called upon by the gracious lady whom we all obey; and I shall call my sketch

THE LAWYER'S STORY.

My tale is a short one, and soon told. The life of a middle-aged and rather rusty lawyer does not incite to much incident to break its monotony. When the event occurred which has been, and will be, the dominant one of my life, I was living in a street about a mile from the immediate city, chosen by me because it was apart. The lack of relatives and friends made me shrink from the numbers of mere every-day acquaintance, and the quiet hours for reading after my day's work, in my remote chambers, were more soothing than the sounds of evening bustle and entertainment which by contrast would have reminded me still more forcibly of my own solitariness. Across the street and opposite my windows there stood far back from the sidewalk an old house, somewhat weather-beaten with its hundred years, and with a charm that often attaches itself to an old building, but with an air of neglect and almost squalor about it. A long flagstone walk, which led to the high steps, was bordered on either side by a tangled garden, in which I sometimes now linger a little ; for even after these many years it has with its subtle odors of box and southernwood the power to lead me back through the cleared paths of memory to that faint-remembered past.

Only a few rooms of the large house were occupied, and these by an elderly lady and her granddaughter and one old servant. The granddaughter, a pretty, fragile child of eighteen, whose chill, unchildlike life had been made as colorless and drooping as the pale white roses in her garden, where I mostly saw her, awoke in me much tender interest, and a sorrow that anything so lovely and so young should be so solitary ; and I found myself instinctively looking forward to her pathetic little smile of welcome as I went my way at morning, and in the coming back at twilight. A few trifling acts of neighborliness on my part to the grandmother had already led to a slight acquaintance, though the stiff formality of the elderly lady did not invite to much intimacy; yet even that bleak background could not altogether prevent the girl's sweet youth from springing up in spite of it, with the same gentle force which sent the snowdrops pushing through the barren earth in the old garden. On my way to my office one fair June morning I saw on the bills that the opera for that evening was to be " Martha," and a sudden impulse emboldened me and made me determine that my little girl should be taken out of her dull surroundings, at least for once, and be gladdened as well as all the rest of the world. I felt almost young as I stole home earlier than my wont — a little guiltily, taking my unusual pleasure somewhat under protest, and went to ask permission of the grandmother. The request was granted, and an hour later we were on our way, and my pleasure had already begun, in seeing a look of expectant happiness on her serious face. The charm of the music of the opera, and the old, old story forever new, deepened the questioning outlook of her grave, sweet eyes. I wandered away in my thoughts from the scenes enacted before me, and made others for myself, wherein she should be the heroine, and a love far tenderer and more passionate than the lover's on the stage should be given to her, and I, whose dull rôle in life was so nearly played out, would be content to be only a looker-on.

The memory of that one festal evening, and the pleasant talks we had afterwards about it, served to fill many an hour of the long hot days, which had now reached into July. The burning sun and drought began to tell strongly on the old garden, its look of desolateness all the greater since I had lately missed seeing the faithful little hand tending the straggling shrubs and stalks, and trying to lure them back into their old grace. Growing somewhat impatient at her continued absence, I stopped one morning at the door to ask for her, and was told by the servant that she was ill, and had for some time been drooping. The doctor whom they called in said that the intensity of the prolonged heat had prostrated her, and that he feared fever. Depressed by the account, I went on to my office, to find there a message from a far-off connection to the effect that I should appear in person in the small town of W. to settle a dispute which had arisen from the will of a relative. It would take me two days to reach there, and as the business to be settled might occupy many more, I must start at once in order to be back in time to meet other engagements. I had only time to hurry to my rooms to make my preparations and be off. There was not much for me to do; a word to the woman who served as housekeeper and servant to look after my few belongings, and I was ready. I should have gone my way with a lighter heart if I could have carried with me a word from my little girl, and could have seen her waiting there with her smile of farewell. I felt selfishly thankful that I was going to new scenes which might help to weaken the sense of sadness.

I had not anticipated pleasure or much interest in meeting with these relatives altogether unknown to me, and so the surprise was agreeable to find myself in the midst of a little colony very hospitably inclined. The business capacity with which I was invested assumed to them in their narrow and local lives a vast importance, and their friendliness made my ten days' stay most pleasant; and in leaving I felt I was not altogether so lonely an object as before. But in the late afternoon of the following day, as I stepped from the station into the noisy town, which seemed unendurably heated and stifling in contrast to the cool quiet of the country, the full weight of solitariness fell upon me. I walked along in the gathering twilight, until the noises became fewer, and the stillness of a deserted city seemed to be brooding. I turned into the familiar street, and in the accustomed way looked up at the house standing gray in the waning light, to discern dimly, perchance, some glimpse of a face which in all that city would be the only one to brighten at my return. Disappointed in not seeing her there, I reached my door, turned the key in the lock, and went up to my room, where the cheerlessness and gloom struck me as never before. I threw open the windows and lighted a candle. A high south-wind was rising, and the draught sweeping through scattered the papers on my writing-table, and I began to gather them together, mechanically sorting them, stopping in my work to listen to a far-off street band, the strains of which were lifted by the wind now and then and brought up to my window. The music was only an old hackneyed air from " Martha," but it sent me back to the bright glad evening I had passed with the sweet, grateful child who might perhaps be still lying ill in that gloomy chamber in the old house. " As soon as I have tied up the papers," I said to myself, " I will go over and find out about her." The wind at that moment blowing open the door behind me, I reached my hand back to shut it, when it resisted my touch and was gently pushed forward. I turned, and there before me I saw her standing. My first impulse was one of relief and joy, for the smile and light which rested on her face told me she was well again. The frank, calm eyes looked into mine, and yet as I tried to meet their look I saw the gaze went far beyond, and in an instant the thought sprang to my brain that she was in the power of somnambulism. Else, why should she be here? Every question vanished before the one compelling desire to keep her from sudden waking, and to lead her safely home. She moved gently round the room, softly sighing, and once she stopped and leaned upon the back of a chair, folding her hands together, and smiling toward me, but not at me. Then, turning, she passed through the open door, out into the long dark passage-way, her white wrappings glimmering faintly before me. Breathlessly I followed her — down into the street. The band was playing still its "Last Rose of Summer," and I trembled in an anguish of fear lest it should waken her. She moved on before me, crossed the street, and turned in at the gate, and along the flagstone walk, then up the long flight of steps.

 I thanked Heaven that thus far she was safe, and stepped in front of her to strike the knocker, when — a light breath of wind lifted something that rose, and fell, and fluttered against the whiteness of her dress. I saw that it was a knot of something black. In terror less the nameless horror which swept through me should reach her too, I turned my head toward her. There was no one there! In a frenzy I struck the heavy knocker, and a whole eternity seemed to roll over me while I waited for the slow footsteps to reach the door.

I was conscious only of gasping her name, and of hearing some one whisper, "She is dead, sir. She died this afternoon."

*Non avéa pur natura ivi dipinto,
Ma di soavità di mille odori
Vi facéa un incognito indistinto.*
                    DANTE, *Il Purgatorio.*

*What if heaven be that, fair and strong
At life's best, with our eyes upturned
Whither life's flower is best discerned,
We, fixed so, ever should so abide !
What if we still ride on, we two,
With life forever old yet new,
Changed not in kind, but in degree,
The instant made eternity, —
And heaven just prove that I and she
Ride, ride together, forever ride ?*
                    ROBERT BROWNING.

FOURTH DAY.

Mrs. Nye came to the White House just after breakfast was over, and found Margaret and her friends sitting under the linden-trees, Mrs. Bowdoin in the hammock, the Professor cutting the pages of the last "Atlantic Monthly," Margaret talking with her brother, who had just come from the stable, Muriel busy with a piece of embroidery, while Charlie Wyatt seemed absorbed in watching the movements of her white hands and deft fingers; Mr. Bowdoin smoked his cigar, and looked as serenely content as did Erin and Joujou. "Quite a stranger! quite a stranger!" remarked Polly in a deep bass voice, which she always assumed when she wanted to be very polite.

"Polly speaks the truth; you have not been to see us for a long time," said Margaret, getting up and going to meet her old friend with outstretched hands. "But your time is too valuable to waste on a parcel of idlers like ourselves, I know."

"Not a bit of it," said Mrs. Nye, smiling all over. "I just admire to come here, and you know that, dear Mis' Temple; but there, I says to father this mornin', 'I have n't been over lately,' says I, 'because it's just here: they're to breakfast about the time I'm gettin' my dinner ready, and then they go off somewheres, and by the time they get back it's my supper-time, and their dinner (though I *did* say, it seemed to me just callin' things out o' their names, but I guess that's because I'm so old-fashioned), and so it goes.' But to-day father wanted me to come and bring you some lovely fresh eggs our hens have just laid, and some butter of my yesterday's churnin', and he wanted me to say to the gentlemen that there's a big school o' bluefish right out in the bay, and he thought they might like to go after 'em. He has n't known 'em be round here so thick for ever so long. He's goin' out in his cat, and he'll be pleased to take any of you with him, if Mis' Temple don't want her boat to get all fished up."

"Tell the Captain, please, that I'll go with him with the greatest pleasure, for one," said Mr. Bowdoin.

The others did not speak for a moment; then Margaret said, "We were just arranging a riding-party when you came, Mrs. Nye. I find that you can ride my mare Magali, Muriel; she hurt her foot slightly last week, but she is all right now. I shall take Cranberry, the horse I usually drive in the phaeton; he is a delightful saddle-horse. You shall have Mahomet Bey, Mr. Kirkland, I know you will like him; and Ralph has his own mare, Black Pearl. I was just consulting with Ralph, Mr. Wyatt, as to whether Hassan Bey, the other one of the pair, would carry you; he's quite a good horse in the saddle, but —"

"Thanks, dear Mrs. Temple," said Wyatt quickly, "you are too good to trouble yourself about me, but I would not spoil the quartet for the world. Tell your husband, Mrs. Nye, that I will hunt the bluefish with joy, in his good company. We will be ready at his call. I must go on board my boat first to give some orders," he added, "so I will bid you ladies good-morning, and wish you a delightful ride. I shall give the Captain and Bowdoin lunch on board the 'Hope,' Mrs. Temple, for I know we shall not be here in time for yours; I have been bluefishing with Tom before to-day." He went towards Muriel, and bending over her said a few words in a low voice; she blushed and looked rather distressed, but said aloud, "Don't forget to bring the song you promised to show me; you said you had it on board your boat."

"I will not forget," he replied, and strode off through the garden, ran down the bank, and was out of sight in a moment.

"Those broad shoulders of Antinous' seem to wear an injured or indignant air," said Mr. Bowdoin, with a look of assumed innocence. "What can be the matter, I wonder!"

When Mrs. Nye had gone, Margaret said, "I am really very sorry about Mr. Wyatt; but five *is* an awkward number, and I knew you would not ride, Bell. As to Tom, when there is a bluefish within reach, there is he in pursuit always. After all, yesterday was Mr. Wyatt's field-day; and perhaps we will go for a moonlight sail this evening, if he asks us. That will settle things nicely." Margaret really looked troubled. She could not bear that every one should not be quite contented and happy; but that is not always possible, even at Fair Harbor.

"What a beautiful creature your mare is!" said the Professor, as he and Margaret struck into the woods, and along the western shore towards Falmouth. "And how did you happen to name her 'Magali'? It is the name of the heroine in 'Mirèio,' is it not?"

"I had a horse at Cannes, years ago," answered Margaret, "that I christened 'Magali.' I read 'Mirèio' there for the first time in the poet's own enchanting country, and in his own tongue, with the help of Miss Preston's delightful translation. So as this horse really looks a good deal like my pretty Provençal favorite, I call her too 'Magali.' We went to Algiers from Cannes, and then to Rome; it was the winter — " Margaret stopped, and her voice faltered — "you remember — "

"Yes," said Kirkland earnestly, "I remember; as if I could ever forget!" And they rode on for some time silently.

Margaret's husband (as has been already said) died in Algiers in the winter of which she spoke. Her brother went out to her and induced her to go to Rome with him, where they remained four months, and where, notwithstanding her seclusion, she saw Professor Kirkland often, as he was an intimate friend of Ralph. She had not seen him from that time until now, for it had always so happened that when Margaret was at home he had been away. He was a great traveller, and had just now returned from a voyage round the world. He had resumed his place at Harvard, and seemed disposed to stay at home for the present. Nothing has been said of his personal appearance, for when Charlie Wyatt was about, his beauty was really so brilliant and so compelling, that it was the main fact in the landscape. Yet Kirkland was a most distinguished looking man, — the sort of man of whom it would always be asked, wherever he went, "Who is he?" He was tall, and strongly built, with dark eyes, very deep and penetrating; his hair and moustache were slightly tinged with gray, but he was in the prime and fullest vigor of manhood. His eyes could put on a very tender look sometimes, especially when he was with little children, of whom he was very fond, and who always worshipped him. He had a rarely beautiful smile, which lighted up what might else have been rather a severe countenance, and a peculiar charm of manner; yet so far as any one knew, he had never cared specially for any woman, and the impression generally prevailed that he never meant to marry.

We will leave them threading the narrow woodpaths, where sometimes the horses had no room to go abreast, and follow Ralph and Muriel, who had chosen other paths to the same end, as the four had promised to meet at Long Pond at a certain hour.

"How wonderful this autumn color is!" exclaimed Muriel, as they came out of the thicket to a piece of undulating ground where pine-trees had been cut down, and where the shrub (or scrub) oak on either side of the road made a rich glow of every shade of scarlet, crimson, and tawny russet among brilliant green leaves.

As far as the eye could reach, there was a very carnival and passion of color. There were hedges of barberry, with leaves stained red, and graceful sprays hung full with coral fruit; golden-rod and purple asters filled the ways; the foliage of the grape-vine was turning amber and orange, and its sweet penetrating scent was more subtle and delicious than wine; bayberry and sweet fern sent up their spicy fragrance like incense crushed out of them as the riders passed.

"Yes, it is marvellous," rejoined Ralph. "Somehow one gets nearer to the color here, one is more thoroughly of it, steeped in it, than in regions where the trees are higher. Margaret calls it taking a color-bath to come here in the autumn; and truly the expression is not bad."

"It seems to me all she says is well said, and all she does is well done," replied Muriel. "I think I have never seen any one I admired so much, or could grow to love more dearly."

"She is a dear creature, certainly," said Ralph heartily, "and the best sister a cranky, half-savage sort of fellow like me ever had, bless her!"

"Indeed," said Muriel, with a little touch of heightened color, and a half-sweet, half-mischievous smile, "I can quite understand what she must be to you, and how happy you are together; and I don't at all wonder that you looked upon the coming of an unknown stranger between you two as a 'horrid nuisance.'"

"Great heaven!" burst out Ralph. "Then you did hear! I was an insensate fool — a brute! But I am well punished. Ah, I beseech you, as you are strong, be merciful! Will you, can you, forgive me? I shall never forgive myself."

Muriel murmured something about there being nothing to forgive, and Ralph went on impetuously, —

"Yes, I was a brute; but, I repeat, I have been well punished. To be near you day after day, and hour by hour, every moment revealing some new charm, some added loveliness, — to grow to watch every movement you make, every word you utter, — to have to see you gracious and kind to others, and to acknowledge to myself that they deserve your favor, while each gentle word you speak to me only makes me hate and despise myself the more, — all this has been a bitter though a merited retribution."

Muriel was going to reply, when Mrs. Temple and the Professor appeared beside them, emerging from the woods, and spared her what might have been an embarrassing moment.

"And here we are by the pond, and near the trysting-tree," said Margaret.

They rode to the edge of the lake, and walked their horses some way into the clear water and let them drink.

"Now we will ride once round the famous oak-tree, and to-morrow we will bring the others here, that those who say there are no big trees on the Cape may be confounded. I have quite forgotten how many feet it measures round its trunk, or round the turf its branches shadow, but I know that a large picnic-party can abide beneath its shade. Would it not be nice to come to-morrow afternoon and let Bell read her story to us here?"

Captain Nye and his wife were in the little garden in front of the farm-house as Margaret and the Professor rode by on their way home. They had parted company again from Muriel and Ralph, who were nowhere to be seen, and the Professor had told Margaret *his* story. It was not a new one; it has been told since the world began, and there shall be never an end to it while the world endures.

He had never cared for any woman but her, and he had loved her ever since he knew her, many years ago. He had not dared to tell her so then, for he "feared his fate too much," and she had had no suspicion. When they were in Rome, after her husband's death, he had tried hard not to let her know the state of his feelings, and had reproached himself severely that he had not always been able to command his tones and speech.

But now! so little while, and the universe was changed! The miracle was worked,— the miracle which those two hearts held as precious, and whose transfiguring power they blessed as fervently, as if it had bloomed upon the earth that day, and never before in all the days and years.

" The long day wanes ; the slow moon climbs; the deep
Moans round with many voices. Come, my friend,
'T is not too late to seek a newer world."

Past we glide, and past and past!
Why's the Pucci palace flaring
Like a beacon to the blast?
Guests by hundreds, not one caring
If the dear host's neck were wried.
           Past we glide.
                               ROBERT BROWNING.

This night I'll spend
Unto a dismal and a fatal end:
Great business must be wrought ere noon:
Upon the corner of the moon
There hangs a vaporous drop profound;
I'll catch it ere it comes to ground:
And that, distilled by magic sleights,
Shall raise such artificial sprites
As by the strength of their illusion
Shall draw him on to his confusion.
                               MACBETH.

It was ordained to be so, sweet! — and best
Comes now, beneath thine eyes, upon thy breast.
Still kiss me! Care not for the cowards!
                               ROBERT BROWNING.

EVENING OF FOURTH DAY.

"DID you lose your way in the woods this afternoon, Ralph?" asked Mrs. Temple, as the brother and sister were sitting in the hall waiting for their guests to come down to dinner. "The Professor and I must have got home fully half an hour before you, and we rode slowly, too."

"No, we did not lose our way," said Ralph, (was it the reflection of the firelight that gave his cheek such a glow?) "but you know Magali's foot had been tender, and I was not sure of her being shod just right, and — and — "

"Ah, Ralph, dear boy, take care, take care! Muriel has been confided to me, and I must have no flirting. Perhaps I should not have let her go on a *tête-à-tête* ride at all. But really, as after all it was a party of four, and as I supposed my brother was to be trusted — "

"Do you mean he is not?" asked Ralph, a trifle indignant. "Surely you do not imagine that I should say a word to Miss Carr-Wynstede to which you or any one could object? Let me see — what did we talk about? You were one of the principal subjects of conversation, as far as I can remember. And we did speak of the autumn foliage. What were you and Kirkland discussing chiefly, if it comes to that? Not my poor self, I'll be bound."

The appearance of the others prevented any more confessions, and all but Mrs. Chauncey were assembled.

"Really, Caroline Chauncey is a trial to those who love her!" exclaimed Margaret.

"Let's sit down without her," said Ralph, "and give her cold ham when she comes."

"At a side table," added Bowdoin.

"Poor, dear Caroline, she sha' n't," said Margaret, becoming soft-hearted and a little incoherent. "We'll wait a little longer. Men are always so impatient, especially for their dinner."

"Ugh!" cried Bowdoin; "how those sand-flies bite! I must have brought them up from the beach."

Early in the week Margaret had been obliged to confess that there was an occasional sand-fly to be seen, or felt, down by the water. "I think there were never any until this year," said she. "Those Philadelphians, the Shallings, brought them. They are charming people, the Shallings, but they must have brought them. They had been at Long Branch before they came here." At this moment she felt her instep was being stung, and she shook her skirts. "Another of those New Jersey sand-flies," she said.

"I'm getting hungry," observed Ralph.

"Mr. Travers must have a great deal of food, I believe," said Miss Carr-Wynstede, "or else he won't be able to get through his story."

"My dear, he shall. Am I not his sister?"

"Pooh!" said Ralph. "I have been hungry under your care before now. Do you remember a dreadful picnic — "

"Ralph," cried Margaret, "New York is making you — slowly but surely — horrid."

"Mr. Travers confessed to me this afternoon," said Muriel, "that he was awfully frightened about to-night."

Charlie Wyatt was standing by himself while the rest were talking, looking out at the open door, through which the evening breezes came softly, blowing odors of honeysuckle into the hall. He might have been thought to be watching for Mrs. Chauncey, being also impatient for his dinner. But it was not so. Mr. Bowdoin had confided to his wife, when he came from fishing, that Wyatt had seemed terribly bored and preoccupied. "He had a fine bluefish on his hook," he said, "and he would n't take the trouble to play him and bring him in; I had to do it for him. And he called me Miss Carr-Wynstede twice. The first time, of course I did n't hear him; but the second, I simply laughed at him. He turned red, and looked very much annoyed, and confoundedly handsome."

The waitress was seen to speak to Mrs. Temple, and was heard to whisper, "The cook says —"

"And I say so too," cried Ralph, jumping up, "in spite of poor dear Caroline!"

"Mr. Kirkland," said Margaret, "what are

A Week away from Time. 185

you reading?" for the Professor had taken a pamphlet from his pocket, and was reading it by the lamp on the hall table. " It looks like a Report. I ought to have warned you that for this week we allow nothing of the kind. I have several waiting for me in the post-office. I refused to take them out."

The Professor put down the pamphlet. " It is a Report of some spiritualistic meetings, sent me by a convinced friend. It contains the account of a young woman in Iowa who removed the furniture of a large drawing-room to the attic in five minutes."

" Well, I should have been furious if they 'd done anything like that in my parlor," said Mrs. Bowdoin.

" Except the grand piano," continued the Professor. " That would not turn a corner in the second staircase. Ten men were employed to get all the things down again the next day."

" Why did n't they make the medium do it herself?" inquired Ralph.

" She was very delicate, and said she could not endure the strain. She is always in bed for a week after these manifestations. She has made five hundred converts in the city of Des Moines alone."

"By Jove!" exclaimed Ralph, "the whole business makes me sick. It is one of the tinsel signs of the times, too. People have read a little Darwin and decided that they cannot swallow the Bible any longer. They let go of Christianity, or have never had hold of it, and go scrambling and diving about for something else. Your baker takes his wife of a Sunday evening to a hall where by paying ten cents they can see a charlatan go into forged epileptic fits, and call it somebody's grandmother; or if they are a little higher up in the scale, or better able to afford it, they pay a dollar, and go to a séance at the South End, where they sit close to one another in the dark, and white forms glide in and out of a cabinet to slow music, and some poor lady among the deluded company is locked in the arms of one of the white forms, and weeps over it with tears of joy, for this her only daughter was lost, and is found again. And a man goes out from the circle and stands

A Week away from Time. 187

for ten minutes holding another of the materialized forms (very much materialized, I am inclined to think) in his embrace, calling her by all manner of endearing epithets. A pitiful exhibition of human weakness and wickedness. As for their esoteric Buddhism, that's simply the latest orchid some of the 'cultured' people have got hold of, to have about on their tables. I'm tired of these bastard rubbishy religions."

"Why, Ralph, how oddly you talk!" said Margaret.

Just then a voice was heard speaking outside. "I couldn't help it. I went up to dress an hour and a half ago; and what do you suppose? I had sent my dresses to Boston this morning, and kept my clothes for the wash here. Now, pray don't laugh, for I did not know what I should do. I thought I might have to stay in bed, until I found this black lace dress in the bottom of my trunk. And I've kept your dinner waiting. My dear, I am so sorry! It's most embarrassing. Such a time as I have had! They'll all be down again to-morrow with the ice-cream. They don't make it at the hotel, you know, and I thought I'd treat the children there. I've telegraphed. I said to Fera, 'Go to house, and get dresses.' I said to them at my house, 'Take dresses to confectioner's.' So they'll all come together by the morning train."

When they were seated at dinner, she said to Ralph, "I hear it is your turn to-night, Mr. Travers. What are you going to tell us about? Venice! Paul knew all about Venice—the piles, you know. Things under the house that let the water into your cellar; but they ought not to. Paul built some houses down on the Back Bay, and they relapsed, or did whatever houses down there do; and he went to Venice afterwards, and found that those old architects knew all about it. He explained to me, I remember; he said the salt water kept the wood from rotting in Venice, and somehow it did n't in Boston. So I decided I'd rather stay where I was, above Charles Street."

After dinner Ralph begged Muriel to sing one song, and he should be better able to read his story; and Muriel sang:—

WHITE DAYS.

Yesterday, not a song in the air,
    Not a hope in the sky,
    No bird on the wing —
A sealed and death-still earth, relentless, bare:
    To-day all the land doth sing!

Yesterday, like a barrier,
    Forcing our lives apart,
The ground lay like a heavy grave:
    To-day the snowdrops start.

Yesterday, an unreckoned space
    Stretched from my path to thine:
To-day, thy hand, thy voice, thy face, —
    All dearest things are mine!

Bell whispered to her sister, — "She puts quite a new expression into her singing to-night. Which of them is it, my dear?" But she saw an unusual expression in Margaret's own face, which was full of emotion, and stopped, a little frightened.

Ralph was now commanded to begin. He cleared his throat, and looked very nervous.

"If you have never been in Venice, it is your loss," he began; "and how great a loss you will never know till you go there. You mustn't yawn, Bell."

"My dear, it was the tone," said his sister, — "so hollow."

"Yes, wasn't it?" said Mrs. Chauncey, "as if he were talking out of the plug in the bath-tub."

"Well, I never told a story before," said Ralph, getting more and more awkward. "Wyatt, why can't you take us on board your yacht? I think I could get on better there. I sha'n't see them yawn so distinctly by moonlight."

This was carried; at last the chairs on deck were comfortably arranged, and cigars puffed. Wyatt sat at Muriel's feet to-night, and was only a passenger. The moon was just rising, the stars shone brilliant in the sky, and a warm smell of sedge filled the air. Ralph took a second start, and began the story of

THE PALACE OF THE CLOSED WINDOW.

THE dining-room of the Three Wise Men of the Orient is a squalid little place. Its waiters are plausible, and they smile continually; this good-nature on their part, however, adds but little savor to the food. If you ask for a bottle of wine, you get something so sour that it files the throat all the way down. The wonder is that you ever ask for another, or that you return to the inn at all. Perhaps the reason that I shall always put up there is because, as I sit in Wall Street, I can close my eyes and see the genial face of the landlord, and think of the two ascending steps that lurk in the blackest part of my bedroom passage. The smell that pervades the premises resembles no other odor I have met. But a smell you know is better than a new smell; therefore in August, 188-, I came back to the Albergo of the Three Wise Men of the Orient. My room, No. 7, was unchanged; its door still swung back on joints that slanted it farther from the floor each inch they opened. On the rumpled white curtain in my window the bodies of mosquitoes I had flattened there the year before still stuck. Her excellency my chambermaid had a thumping tread, and was shrill-voiced of a morning, but she was very glad to see me. "Eh, my lord, how does the Signorino do?" said she; and she remembered to put an additional green pail of water in my room. Moreover, the leaky seam in my tub had been soldered. This the grinning Sebastiano pointed out as he lugged it into its corner. I found such discomfort comfortable. The very tune the man in the alley-way behind still played on his clarinet after some twelve months beat a rhythm grateful to my ear, — for the first day, at least. At dinner the usual food was served. The waiter, Antonio, smiled as he bent over with his dishes, as much as to say, "The Signore will recollect our ambrosia. Nothing in the world like it!" There was nothing in the world like it, so the Signore recollected very well. Pah! how delightfully bad it was! And here was Venice again, to be sure; and in the Signore's pocket was a bundle of letters for the American Colony; they had been consigned to him by various Americans who persisted in dwelling in the States. They promised tedious hours. Bunched together next my heart, though with several thicknesses of stout English cloth between, they felt bulky enough to support a season of gloves and white cravats. I spread them on the table after my soup was removed; I had to push the glasses and salt-cellars about, to make room for them. I looked at them, and through them to the other side, into a vista of card-plates and

The Palace of the Closed Window. 193

open doors, where voices of servants told me their mistresses were at home.

One letter was to a venomous little lady who had once lived in Thirty-eighth Street, New York. She would dine me, and after dinner, over her liqueurs and cigarettes, she would inquire what color I preferred her hair, and would regale me with anecdotes; these would bear the cosmopolitan stamp. Another letter was to a family of three seedy daughters and their old fustian papa. He trailed them from Venice to Rome, from Nice to Pau and Paris, and so back to Venice. All were accomplished. Emilie sang Tuscan street-songs to the guitar; Lizzie tinkled the zither and yodled Styrian ditties with an accent pronounced amazing by those who knew; Maria sang "Le petit bleu," "Elle a du zut, zut, zut," and once in a while after supper she could be persuaded to dance while her two sisters twanged the guitar and piano and the guests rattled the fire-irons. Every one said these girls preserved their "entrain" wonderfully. Then other letters to colony painters lay before me,— young men who deplored the future of art in America, and spoke fluently the jargon of the ateliers. Must this correspondence be presented for civility's sake? I stared gloomily into space, till my eye rested on the single other guest of the Three Wise Men, and he grew bleared under my blank scrutiny. I did not know that he had for some time been staring at me with all his might.

"Lieber Gott! and is it my friend Travers?" he exclaimed, tipping over his chair as he hurried up from his end of the table.

I recognized the excellent Caspar Zell. "Why, Caspar! Why, bless my soul! Why, how did you crawl into this place?"

"And is it not more likely, Mr. Broker from Wall Street, that I, the artist, the 'Farbenmeister,' should nose out a little hole like this? Waiter, another bottle of red wine! Aha, Mr. Broker! we'll set some of the juice trickling down our throats, eh?"

"Sir, to you! But what are you doing here?"

"Doing? My box is not yet unpacked. I am come to-day from Vienna for a change."

"How goes work?"

"Excellent. I hang in Munich for the whole world to admire me, and two pictures have I sold in Dresden. One is — pst! not very serious. I call it 'Hearing Strauss.' Of course it is a man with his girl. And you?"

"Excellent also. I do not hang anywhere yet."

"And the philosophy, Herr Broker? Are we as practical and 'wirklich' as ever? Do we still scoff at the truth-seekers?"

"We still do, Caspar. Money-making, plain thinking, and high living remain our little all, bless them!"

"Ach! you New York humans are astonishing, with your street of ticking-machines, and your church at the end like an Amen. Do the Midases of the Republic go there after business to rinse the gold out with a cupful of holy water, so it will be quite fresh for dinner? Ach, a versatile people!"

"I guess we're versatile, Caspar, but we ain't much like that."

"Now you drawl, and talk with your practical nose. Another bottle will give you a good temper; you will feel ready for some philosophy. No? Well, then, come out into the town. You have no notion how I am glad to see you once more." And taking my arm he hurried me into a gondola and away, talking continuously. "Ach!" he began, "let no one speak to me of the mystery of night elsewhere. Look up at those passing walls; we feel more than we see. Is it not as if they were scenery in the back of a theatre? Have you ever gone behind the stage when dusk was coming? When you are next at Weimar, I will take you. It makes a wonderful effect on the nerves."

"The nerves, *your* nerves, you Teuton?"

"And why not my nerves, adopted son of Wall Street?"

"Why, Caspar, I thought you were a materialist."

"I am a materialist, — a hundred times a materialist; but what of that? Because I know that what we call fear is nothing but a vibration of nerve tissue, can I stop my particular tissue from vibrating? At any rate, we Germans have imagination; and I believe you Americans have none at all."

I found I had enough to keep me silent as the walls glided by. The unfrequent lamps served to show buildings that might rise to unlimited heights and descend to depths equally quiet and unfathomed.

"What are the half-dozen lighted cafés and piazzas in such a universal hush as this?" I mused aloud.

"The Past, she is queen here still, nicht wahr?" said Caspar. "These walls, these walls; things have been acted behind them. Let us get into the light and have a glass of something!"

We had several glasses of something. The buzz of the café, and the cheerful haste of waiters tinkling the glasses they carried, put a new aspect on the city. Caspar and I soon arranged our programme. Three weeks were to be given to Venice, — he to sketch, and both of us to loaf; and then we should walk in the Salzkammergut. I sauntered to the water with a glass in one hand and my letters in the other. "There," I said, dropping them in, — "there goes the American

Colony. I come from an American Colony, and one's enough. Caspar, I shall expect you to give me points on 'Renaissance,' and 'Décadence,' and all the rest of it, and I'll tell you when I see a girl worth painting."

"Agreed, Herr Broker," said Caspar. "Now to the hotel."

We got into our gondola, and turned from the broad water, in which lights were twinkling, into a narrower passage that curved into the gloom. The sombre walls began to put forth their influence again. But Caspar had become musical, and was now uttering a string of fragments in a deep and somewhat harsh bass.

"Where rippling waters rise and fall,
    And boats glide silent 'neath each palace wall,"

he sang.
            " Where love is plenty
                For two-and-twenty,"

chimed in another voice from the water's edge, — a man's voice, but mellow as the night wind. "Ho! my friends. You sing good songs. In the name of your music, do me a great favor. I am caught in a mesh, and cannot reach my destination by land. I have hailed gondolas in vain. Set me down, in all charity beyond the second bridge from here, and I am at your service."

"Go under the lamp, then, and show us what for a man you are," said Caspar.

"Nonsense, Caspar; we'll take him," I said, laughing.

"The request is fair," said the voice, but somewhat haughtily. In a moment he stood under the lamp, which shone quietly down on him. Leaning back against the wall, he was all of six feet; but standing, he would have gained an inch at the least. Over one arm hung a cloak; the other was akimbo. We could see he had a slight black moustache, and a chin clean cut and pointed. The upper half of the face was in shadow.

"Well?" he asked, laughing a little, as we continued to eye him.

"Step in, sir, by all means," I hastened to say.

"It is true I am armed," he continued, "but I am one and you are four."

Caspar was still silent. The stranger now laughed outright. He made a gesture.

"There!" he said, as something clattered in the bottom of the boat.

I stooped and picked up an exceedingly beautiful stiletto.

"Now I am at your mercy, you see," continued our would-be guest.

We bumped against the side, and he stepped in, light and true as a wild animal.

"I own," said he, "that such a request as mine was a trifle out of the common; but I felt sure you would grant it when I heard your music. I have always found that the carouser who puts a certain free stroke into his songs will give and take a favor easily. Though it was you, sir, I believe, whom I had the pleasure of hearing," he added, turning to Caspar.

"Oh, my dear sir —" began poor Zell.

"Not a word, and no offence. Even the night carouser should be prudent. This corner is not a place to take a stranger on board without stopping to look at him."

We turned into the canal on which was our inn. On the corner stood a palace that in the daylight I had observed as being singularly stately for this quarter of Venice.

"Many thanks," said the stranger; "I will leave you here. No, do not stop the boat." He sprang out as lightly as he had entered. "You have my stiletto. Keep it; *though you will remember me without it!*" and he laughed strangely. Some corner near us reverberated out of the dark. "No, I insist upon your taking it. You are at the Three Wise Men?

We shall meet again, gentlemen, for Venice is small, and I am always at your service; good-night!"

We moved into the shadow, and we thought we heard a door close. There was one that gave entrance to the small garden adjoining the palace.

"H'm! strange person!" observed Caspar. "A practical joker."

"Practical jokers don't make you presents in New York," said I.

"Were I not a materialist, I should say, 'Beware of it!'" replied the artist.

In my room, I examined the weapon carefully. It was certainly an old one, and of most intricate and curious ornamentation. I slipped it into the sheath again, and blew out the light, half expecting it to be gone in the morning. I awaked at a decent hour. The stiletto was on my table, substantial enough to have comforted Macbeth. The clarinet was tooting nasal ditties in the back alley, and Stella, my chambermaid, was screaming cheerfully up and down the passage.

At breakfast Caspar informed me that he was sure he had seen our eccentric guest before — where, he puzzled over without success. But he would know the next time. On our way to sight-seeing (and in Venice it is certainly lions one expects to see) we stared up from the gondola at the palace with the garden wall. Singular that a spider's web across the doorway should be dusty already! There was no other door, nor did the windows show signs of light existing behind them.

"Tell us, friend Luigi," I said to our gondolier, a most amiable and worthless youth, "what that palace is we are passing."

"Signore, we call it the 'Palazzo della Finestra chiusa.'"

"That is a curious name."

"Look, Signore, before we get too far. There, above the row of columns, above the noble story, the line of windows is one too short. Do you see? The cornice juts out, and there is carving on the stone above it, like the others. But the window itself has been walled up."

"Why was that done, Luigi?"

"Who knows? It has always been so, Signore. They are a great family that live there, but they come seldom. 'Forestieri' have tried to hire the palace, but they are always refused. Some of our other patricians are not so particular."

"Now, Luigi, look here! When the family is away, is their house ever visited, or used for any purpose?"

"Eh? no, Signore. What could one do with it? Though I have peeped into the garden myself once or twice. But no one ever walks there. It would not be a bad place for two to take a walk in!" and Luigi kissed his hand fervently at the air.

"Ah, Luigi, you're a rogue, I fear. What does the garden look like?"

"All grown full of flowers and trees, Signore. The trees you can see. They have become tired of their garden, and now look over the top of the wall; so they can listen to what the couples are whispering as they go by of an evening. The flowers, poor things! remain inside." Then our gondolier fell to singing to himself.

As we crossed the Piazzetta, the good natives turned to have a second look at us — or rather at Caspar. I was only an American consulting his guide-book; but Caspar was worthy of attention. The toes of his shoes were wrinkled and square, their heels high and pointed; his hat was of green straw, nearly as tall as a beaver, and his gray coat bulged wherever it could bulge, save at the waist only, where it shrank him into something deserving footlights and a character song. Out of a tail-pocket there invariably stuck a volume of fat German learning, while alongside it rattled a protruding spectacle-case that shifted as he walked, as if struggling to get itself into a comfortable position. The trousers matched the coat; and such was his wear, out of his bedchamber. His night apparel I never ventured to see. I looked up from my Baedeker to watch him wave his admiring hand at the Lagoon and San Georgio, around which the tide was quietly swimming. Then I continued my search in Baedeker for the Palace of the Closed Window.

"Is your guide-book failing you? Perhaps I may be of assistance!"

Of course it was our friend of the stiletto who spoke. There he was, smiling courteously. He walked toward me, and jumped over an intervening chain that stretched between some stone posts. Sunlight showed him to be a man as much out of the common as he had seemed at night. As he came up, I measured him with my eye and concluded that his parting with the stiletto would have availed me very little if it had come to that. Caspar had turned, and was looking at him in obvious perplexity.

"Good-morning, Signore — Signore — "

"Giulio; Giulio Massano," he replied. "But you are looking for something in the book?"

"Yes," I answered slowly, "and I cannot find it."

"Perhaps I can help you. I am as familiar with Venice as though it were my home." By this time my answer was concocted. "I was trying to learn," I said, "the reason that Titian offered the Signoria his services in a piece of work for four hundred ducats, when Perugino had refused double the sum twenty years before."

At the name of Titian there happened a curious circumstance. Caspar struck one fist into the other, and stared harder than ever, while the dark eyes of young Giulio (he seemed not twenty-five) had for one second a terrible look, and the muscles of his jaw knotted under his cheeks. He had noticed Caspar's action also, and gave him a quick glance, anything but friendly.

"Caspar is getting eccentric, too," I thought. "I shall soon be doing something extraordinary myself."

"*Titian!*" said the Italian violently. Something choked him. He cleared his throat. "Titian was a money-dredging traitor! That is—to his art, you understand, sir."

Caspar plunged into a hot defence of the painter.

"Do not let us have an argument," Giulio interrupted, sweeping away any more words with his hand. Then he began to laugh. "You appear to have hit a prejudice of mine," he said to me.

Caspar stole a look at me, and tapped his forehead. But Giulio saw him. "No doubt you think so," he said. "I have been told so before now;" and he gave a grim smile.

All three of us began to walk along slowly. We strolled into St. Mark's, then across to the Ducal Palace. I told myself that all this promised better than the American Colony. I am not yet enough of a confirmed broker to require the stimulus of a New York newspaper in whatsoever part of the world I find myself. My eight weeks in Europe refresh me most when I pass them without hearing a word of American spoken. None certainly was spoken on this morning, which grew stranger as it went on. Giulio — or Julian, as Caspar and I found ourselves calling him without being able to help it — became our guide.

"Red books cannot show Venice to you," said he. "What do they know of the things that lurk here?"

He led us by degrees into the remote corners of the city. It was not churches nor picture-galleries he cared to show us; they were treated as matters of course, though he was evidently as proud of them as if they were his own. But they bored him. The dislike he showed for everything well-known was curious. "They are stranger-ridden, their bloom is gone," he said. "Steam and hotels are turning Venice into a courtesan; she is at money's command." He pointed out the sites of gaming-halls and rioting dens, once flourishing, now extinct. "Here is where much young blood came to no good," said Julian. "But the volcano is not active any more." We descended into a dark hole whose walls were blistered with damp, but still plainly showed that they had been gorgeous in their day. It was a haunt where all young Venice had been used to swarm. We stumbled after Julian through ragged suites of rooms where the wine had once been spilt; the tide-ooze was in them now. As we listened to Julian's talk, the nineteenth century began to dwindle and shrink; the world of modern inventions became separated from our existence, and its thoughts dissolved out of our heads. We followed through by-ways and corridors, down curving flights of stone, sometimes beneath the surface of the water, and again emerging into some nook of masonry. We looked out through barred windows at glimpses of columns supporting invisible roofs, and foliage cloaking their mysterious bases. The spell grew, until time and space and ourselves were as a single mazy vision.

Crossing a balcony, the air became full of whirring and flapping. It was the hour the pigeons were fed, and a cohort of them was leaving the crevices and perches all about us. But to our ears this sounded like an exodus of spirits. Julian's knowledge of every corner was marvellous. From the vagabond side he now turned to the great houses of Venice, and penetrated places virgin to the visits of outsiders. If a

The Palace of the Closed Window.

hidden door were proof against him, he found an accessible spot in the wall. My fear of stewards and custodians soon changed to a relish for our unusual proceedings. We climbed into windows, and we crawled under low arches into forbidden ground.

"We shall at least be in prison together," panted Caspar, as I lifted him up to a ledge that was too much for him.

"I suppose a man could do this, if he chose, in New York or Boston, at certain seasons. During those weeks when front doors on Beacon Street are boarded up to keep them dry, why should not an energetic tourist make his way into three quarters of them from the little ash-barrel lane that runs behind them along the water's edge?"

The great people whose mansions we entered on this most fantastic morning were out of town, and we passed unchallenged. The living-apartments of the Wartburg, or the chambers of Chenonceaux, where lived Diane de Poictiers, are full enough of ghostly history; but the sanctuaries into which we came outdid them all, — family chapels from which the faint odor of incense pervaded the winding approaches to them, on their altars missals colored by the hand of some ancestress, sometimes a shrine set up to a family saint on some family crisis. There were rooms that seemed darkened to keep family secrets closer; sleeping apartments with unexpected doors hard by the bed; galleries from whose walls looked portraits never seen but by friends and descendants; antechambers contrived for listening. In what part of the town we were it was idle to imagine. We never followed a canal or an alley. Sometimes we crossed one, but our way was through bits of garden, narrow passages, up stairways and turrets into galleries running through the thickness of the wall, across covered bridges, in and out, till the place became another Venice. No sign of life disturbed us. At last we came into a long hall and saw ahead of us a white-haired old fellow in a velvet gown. A chain hung from his girdle, and at its end were keys that chinked feebly as they swung in the folds of his robe.

"No harm in him," said Julian. "He is deaf as a post. There he goes into the chapel," he continued. "His ancestor with one of those keys unlocked Sansovino and let him out. Ha! do you know why they shut up Sansovino thirty feet or so beneath where we stand? Because he built some arches in the Library so ill that the ice in the springtime crumbled them. If architects were served so now they would still make good buildings. When we flourished at the expense of our inferiors, the world was a finer place to live in."

"Perhaps that is still being done. The 'lower classes' are still flourishing at the expense of their inferiors." Caspar Zell put a sour emphasis on "lower classes."

Julian stared down at him; the artist stood barely five foot six in his highest heels. "Let us come in here," was all he said.

He pushed open a door that we had not noticed. The floor upon which we entered was of marble. From the ceiling a lamp shone down with dim rays. There seemed to be no other means of light anywhere in the apartment. Thick Eastern stuffs were spread in lieu of carpet, but not so as to conceal the stone altogether, which was of exquisitely pure grain. In a recess stood a bed, also covered with rich materials.

"This lamp has burned three hundred and fifty years," said Julian in a hollow voice. "No one has slept here since the day it was lighted."

The room had been also a living-room. In one corner stood a couch, and by its side a distaff from which dangled a yellow shred. I noticed two little embroidered slippers half hid under the couch. Julian's glance fell on them, and he shuddered and turned away. A silence of the grave fell around us, while with a quickened tread he visited every corner, struggling visibly with some deep emotion. His gait had become agitated and uneven, and we could hear the long breaths he took. In the midst of all this increasing mystery I could not help noticing one curious trifle, — though Caspar and I made constant creaking in our movements, Julian's steps always fell without a sound. But what he was doing, or might do next, had long passed the point of wonder or surmise. I allowed myself to drift on, as if I were contemplating myself from a distance. Julian was now bringing something in his hand.

"See!" he whispered. It was a small harp, whose frame was carved with the legend of Orpheus. Julian seated himself on the couch, and slid his fingers over the strings, which answered with faint, sweet tones. He continued to touch them at random, till gradually a prelude became distinct out of the general harmonious murmur. It came into my head that the sound might bring some one, but if it should, he would probably become merely another actor in all this. Julian had begun to sing, —

> "Should sleep assail thy drowsy eyes,
> When the black priest preacheth wearily,
> Look where the lofty pillars rise,
> And I'll be there to see.
> Oh, wake! and look where the pillars rise,
> And I'll look back at thee.

"When in the hush of placid night
   Lonely I rest, and far from thee,
Speed me thy thought in a vision's flight,
   To be my company.
Dream me some message in the night,
   For all my dream is thee.

"When quiet on my last cold bed,
   I 'm borne, shouldst thou then pass by me,
Draw near and kiss the face of the dead,
   And I 'll rise up for thee.
Whisper my name, and kiss the dead,
   And I 'll wake with a kiss for thee."

The dreary sounds of the harp lingered a moment, then ceased as they had begun, in sweet random chords. Julian silently replaced the instrument. A gust of wind in the corridor rattled the latch. For a moment I expected the old velvet fellow. But nothing entered save the draught, which set some tapestry swinging. Julian stopped it, and lifted a narrow and very delicate strip to show us. The colors were wonderfully blended, and the whole of a surpassing fineness.

"Such work as this is wrought no longer," said he. "A man comes, and glues machine paper on your wall. She who lived here made this piece. What is any contrivance of wheels and levers compared with the wit in one of her little hands?"

He passed his own hand gently over the fabric, and I saw how it trembled. "Let us go," he said. We preceded him into the corridor, but I saw him bend and kiss the embroidery as he turned to follow us out. In the daylight Caspar gave a sigh, and began to assert himself.

"It is all very fine, tapestry and palaces; but there was much of bad going on,—oppression, kings, and open dissoluteness."

Again I saw a look of menace cross Julian's face.

"To-day is better, you would say?"

"Why not? Think of where we are in enlightenment and world-understanding! Was there ever an age like the present?"

"The present! What is the present?"

"Critique, reason, science, mechanique, truth!" and Caspar stood on his toes.

"Truth! If what you say were truth, the world would have nothing left. Hunting truth may be good; but what cares a man for the deer when the chase is over? Truth does not exist. Anything is true."

Caspar gasped at him, and he continued,—

"The mechanical present! A noble time! Men fight each other ten miles apart, and let chemistry make their women's portraits."

"We have also painters now," said Zell, swelling. "Kings and Queens are gone, to be sure."

"You think you are rid of them? They sit in the gutter now, instead of on thrones. You have only placed them elsewhere."

"If that is so, it is a gain. More prosperity is now spread in towns and villages."

"What do we care for spreading prosperity? Is it a glorious thing for a country to swarm with second-class people? The vermin would never have been begotten but for machinery. A noble species, the machine-made citizen! When a man's title to foot it here depended on this,"—and Julian struck his right arm,—"blood ran thicker in his body. When you ran him through, a richer stream spurted out."

"My friend, you were born too late," said Zell.

"You are lucky to have been born when you were," said Julian.

"What is the use in comparing centuries?" replied Caspar.

"None, certainly. But when you say 'critique,'— how many of your little commentators will be known, think you, in the twentieth century? Venice's creators are living still."

"All this is nothing, nothing; merely toys for children," Zell retorted, forgetting that he himself was down in the Weimar directory as an artist. "What is the finest work of art you can show me, compared to a well-fed and enlightened family?"

"What is all this talk compared to lunch?" said I.

Julian put his hand on my shoulder. "Wise man," he said, laughing. But he would not come with us. He brought us out on to the canal, and pointed to the right. "There lies your way," he said. He was leaning against the wall as we had first seen him under the lamp. The gloom had left his manner and voice, which was now that of the vigorous and careless young animal that he looked. I watched him with admiration. But for their delicacy, his features suggested nothing but perfect enjoyment of the five senses. "Till we meet again," he said, and was gone at once.

"A hot-blooded young sinner," I remarked to Caspar.

"Ach! I cannot comprehend such people. He is fierce against all the peaceable rights of the human. Did you see him when he talked about locking architects up? He would do worse than that."

"Perhaps so. A good many worse things might be done, Caspar."

"Himmel!" said he; "look where we are!"

We were standing beneath the Palace of the Closed Window.

The Palace of the Closed Window. 215

"Well, now I suppose we know how some of it looks inside," I said.

"Mr. Travers, Mr. Travers, that young man is a villain!" exclaimed Zell. "If we go with him so again, he will get us into trouble."

"We're not worth robbing, you know, Caspar."

"No, but he will rob, and we shall be caught. That is what I think. What business has any man to know so much about other men's houses?"

"He is not that sort of person," I said. "He is a gentleman, whatever else he may be."

"A gentleman! a fine one, truly! Lock up architects, call decent people vermin, murder citizens to see how thick is their blood; that is a gentleman! I would not trust my safety to him; I would not trust my purse with him; I would not risk my wife or my daughter in his company. He is the worst species of human produced. A gentleman!" And the little painter bubbled and squeaked. "Ach! I almost forgot!" he continued presently. "What in the world put Titian and the ducats into your head?"

"It happened to be the last sentence I had read in the guide-book."

"But do you not know it was very strange of you to say that? I said I had seen his face before. I was wrong. But I have seen one of his kin. Follow me,

Herr Travers. You go to the Louvre; you stop for one moment to look over the shoulder of the old man who paints the Gallerie d'Apollon, and never another thing. He sits at the door of the Salon Carré.[1] Do you know? Well, go in at that door, and (if you can help it) do not turn on your right to look at the Mona Lisa. Go on through the opposite door into the long room. There on your left — is it the second or the third picture? — is a Titian, wonderful, *prachtvoll*, a master-work!"

"Ah! now I know what you're talking about," said I.

"Do you not see the resemblance, even though it is an older man? His hair is black, and his eye too. Has he not also a slight moustache curling round the lip? But he is not in good spirits, like the young Julian. He is like an older and more sinister brother. Yet I could think that Julian might look like that some morning when he lay thinking of what he had done the night before. No; it is more than *Katzen-jammer* with the man in the Louvre. When Titian painted that man, he sat before the master with gloomy thoughts that did not go away with his headache. He thinks — but life does not please him. He, too, is a gentleman, — the same breed. He could also live well at

---

[1] And sits there now (1887) nearly a hundred years old, still copying the Gallerie d'Apollon. — ED.

the expense of his inferiors, and put people that were in his way into dungeons. And he could smile on a woman till she let him betray her. Ach! I hate them all! But they are so beautiful, — and so fine! A race that did everything except be useful. This Julian will look like that picture some day, when seeing too many dawns has given him a pale face. I should like to paint him, once in to-day's dress, and then in costume, with a gauntlet and black cloak and all the rest. And look you, Herr Travers, his name is not Massano. If we knew the name of the man in the picture, we should be able to call Mr. Julian by a name that would make him jump."

There was something in Zell's theory. I have seen folks who resembled the old portraits on their walls. Julian's face was fuller and browner, and he had a most genial laugh. I had certainly seen him look anything but genial, however. Caspar's curiosity to paint his theory had now got the upper hand with him, and he talked of nothing else for several days. During these we found ordinary sight-seeing so flat that we gave it up and took to modern Venice, the Lido, the cafés, queer dances, and night prowling. We saw nothing of Julian, and a strange idleness took possession of Caspar. He sketched nothing. When I spoke of this, he gave as his reason that seeing so much art everywhere was like drowning in one's favorite wine. "The idea of a palette nauseates me," he said. The pianos were going in every direction, as Venice pianos do. Probably a barcarolle a day was constructed on each one. But this energy only disgusted Caspar the more. "It is swill-tub music they make," he said. Then he wandered away, and I did not see him till evening. A change had come over him, and he was eager and restless. "I have seen him again," he began at once, "and now I know that there is something wrong about him. When he saw me, he was not friendly. He asked for you, and did not chat with me at all. But I came direct to the point. I said I wished very much to paint him, and when I said that, he turned and looked at me. *Then* he looked like the portrait! 'For what reason do you honor me so much?' he asked. And when I saw his eye I could not answer. I said I do not know what; and then he bade me good-evening. But he shall not escape me," Zell burst out vigorously. "I shall paint him yet. You will see." And he wagged his head slowly, and looked vastly foolish. "He has an evil conscience, Herr Travers, and feels I suspect him."

I began to grow uneasy about all this. It was evident that Julian was no angel, and might let most principles go at any moment that he found them in-

The Palace of the Closed Window.

convenient. But this was not all. Strangely agreeable as I had found his company, I found myself now thinking with Caspar that "something was wrong about him." The next morning we came upon him sitting on the edge of a quay, fast asleep.

"He has spent the night away from his bed," said Caspar. "Hist! come into this corner, and I will make now his likeness."

"Oh, I think not," I replied.

"And why, pray?"

"Since he objects!"

"Nonsense!" said Zell.

"Well; only remember that you'll be stealing a gentleman's likeness," I said, walking away. Certainly I was not going to assist at this larceny from the person. The artist made no further answer but a grunt, as he angrily took out his materials. Perhaps it was our talk; perhaps it was the sun which now came from a cloud and blazed down on the sleeper's face; but certainly at the first stroke of Caspar's pencil, Julian started to his feet. The pencil rattled out of Zell's hand to the ground, and the paper fluttered away.

"You are devoted to your art, sir, indeed!" was all the Italian said. But it was enough to make Caspar stare wretchedly at him. I hastened to call out a loud good-morning from where I stood.

"Good-morning," Julian answered. "Advise your friend to take better care of himself. Sad things may still happen to painters as well as architects, in Venice, occasionally." He bowed to me, and was gone.

Zell seemed crazed on the subject. Though I saw that no sense of impertinence would detain him, a sense of danger might, I thought. But I was wrong. All day Caspar muttered: "I must have his face. I must have his face. It would be my fortune."

Our stay in Venice was drawing to a close, and my hope was to get Caspar away before he had a chance to commit some new folly. This was not to be. I awoke with an unpleasant start early one morning, and found the Weimar artist at my bedside, with a haggard and vacant expression. I sprang out of bed. "In God's name, what is the matter?" I cried.

"Safe, safe!" was all he could answer. Then he sank into a chair and steadied himself by its arms. Presently he began, —

"I could not sleep. When light dawned I walked out. I went along the edge of the canal till I stood opposite the garden. The spider's web was there, I could see. Over the wall the tree-branches were nodding, nodding. I grew very cold watching them, and so I walked under the closed window. 'Perhaps he

The Palace of the Closed Window. 221

sits inside with the harp now,' I said. I waited, and listened, and peeped on every side; but all was very quiet, and no one was stirring. I thought I might as well turn homeward. I turned, and he was there, leaning against the wall behind me."

Zell's hands shook as he gripped the arms of the chair tighter. "I could not lift my feet, and I thought the air was all going in black waves. He did not move, and I could not take my eyes from his face. His smile was so wicked! He only said, 'You make a poor spy.' He let me stand there till I tried to scream, but I could not. Then he said, 'Do you suppose I would touch you? Crawl home now; you are not hurt. Paint some pictures *if you can*.' His black eyes flashed, and his face — ach! hell was in it. I felt as if something broke in my head. He saw I feared to pass him, and walked swiftly ahead of me, and so round a corner. When I came to the corner I dared not pass it. I walked on my toes as near to the water as I could, and rushed by with all my strength. A horrible laugh rang in my ear. I do not know how I find myself here."

For the last days Caspar Zell would not go anywhere without me. "Let us get away," he said. "I shall not feel right till we are far, far in Salzkammergut, — streams rushing instead of these stagnant canals, and pine-trees in place of walls; and how sweet German speech will sound!"

He never spoke of Julian without his voice becoming husky. For my part, it did not seem to me that Caspar had suffered any hurt beyond a severe fright; his liberties might easily have provoked a worse punishment. Yet though Julian had evidently scorned to retaliate on so little a man, our visit to Venice still seemed to have grown more and more sinister since the first evening. A stiletto would be a fitting thing to remember it by. All the artist seemed to have left Zell. His attemps to sketch were futile.

"I am become paralyzed," he bitterly complained. "Can you remember how his hair went over his forehead? Was it not so?"

"Not at all," I replied. "That face you are making is merely a copy of the one in the Louvre. Young Julian is swarthy, not pale; and you are giving him straight hair."

All day long Caspar spoiled sheets of his album in vain. Finally our heavier effects were sent to wait for us at Munich, and the last day came. We dedicated it to Torcello, whither we were rowed by two gondoliers. As I stretched out in the boat, the stiletto fell from my pocket.

"Why do you carry that?" inquired Caspar.

"To show to a dealer when we get back. I want to find something about it if I can."

The sky was cloudless, and the water rippled blue beneath it; but behind this sereneness lurked a foreboding I could not shake off. We both fell into silences, and I doubt if we could have told what we saw in the Church of Santa Fosca, and the two or three other places we wandered into. We sat for a long time in the bell-tower of the old Cathedral. The swallows dodged about, and took care of their second brood, and in the distance lay the Adriatic and the blue mountains. Then we descended and strolled into the Cathedral. A few shabby candles were lighted on the altar, and a shabby second-best service was performing. The puppets on the steps below bobbed and changed places, while a venerable puppet spun out Latin words with incomprehensible swiftness and incoherence.

"See in the guide-book who is buried here," said Caspar, stopping at a tomb in one of the remoter nooks. "The letters are effaced, but see what a beautiful girl's head! It is an exquisite little carving; and there was another bust beside it, but it is also knocked off."

There was but little light in here, and I stooped to reach a ray that came from one of the candles. My pocket gaped, and the stiletto rang on the pavement.

"Pardon me, sir," said a young priest at my elbow. He handed me the weapon, and the candlelight flashed on it. "What a beautiful one, sir! You are fortunate in having such a curiosity. Do not let an antiquary take it in his hands; you will hardly get it away from him!"

He smiled, and moved noiselessly away. Unable to find information about the tomb, we went out into the air again. But Caspar had now one of his strange fits of restlessness. He talked about the girl's face, and the companion bust that was gone.

"Some one should know about such a work of art," he repeated. "There is our young priest again."

He joined us, and talked very pleasantly. He pointed out various bits we had overlooked in different parts of the island.

"I hope we are not on your hands," I said at length, for we had been walking and talking for about an hour.

"My dear sir, it is so seldom to find agreeable guests at Torcello."

I had come to be sure this was a man of refinement. We talked on many subjects, and none of them were religious ones. His historical knowledge of Venice was most ample and minute, and he delighted to dwell on Venice. I looked at him with increasing interest.

His was no dull eye, nor did he seem able to compass the typical priest's smile in all its wily completeness. Perhaps he had not been long consecrated to the service of Mother Church. But his age I could not tell; he might be twenty-five, he might be forty. His figure was small and slender, but he walked with an elastic step. Yet these lingering suggestions of the flesh did not go with the rest of the man. His face was transparent, and there was an unearthly sadness in his voice. The black dress hung upon him sombre enough for a pall, yet he did not seem a man doomed by disease. I was constantly struck with the liberality of his ideas. At length it became time to go, but Zell spoke up, —

"Perhaps, sir, you could tell us something of a tomb we saw in the Cathedral."

"I can," said the priest; "but it is not often told."

I thought Zell looked as if he were going to say something about money; so I said quickly, —

"I know we are profane tourists; but could you not match my stiletto with a story equally rare?"

"Perhaps, perhaps; yes, *for the sake of the stiletto* I will. To him that hath—" He turned back to the Cathedral without ending the quotation. "Come with me."

We found ourselves again by the tomb. The service was over, the puppets gone; no one now but a lonely old woman kneeling in a corner.

"The tomb is in memory of two, as you see," said the priest; "but only one lies beneath. Is she not beautiful? How sweet a mouth! Has she not a divine face? One would say a saint."

"What was the sculptor's name?" asked Zell.

The priest turned to him with a sad smile.

"Sir, I cannot tell you. He is one of the children whom the father Time has baptized 'Ignoto.' But we know that her name was Margaret. She was not a Venetian. Perhaps you may have seen in the city a palace with one of the upper windows walled up. Yes? That is where Margaret lived, though it was not her home. Sit down on that ledge and I will tell you about her. You remember that our great Titian went to Rome and Florence, and returned here more glorious than when he set out. His wife had died, and he seemed greatly aged by it, for a man of his vigor. I think it was just as well she never knew what a wretch the son she had brought into the world turned out."

"Who?" I asked.

"Her son Pomponio,—a miserable villain. Titian brought a young girl back with him. Who she was exactly, people never knew. He called her Margaret, and people said she was his own granddaughter, Pomponio's child. He never allowed her to see Pomponio, at any rate. Pomponio had become a priest. She called Titian 'godfather,' and whenever he stayed in the houses of great people (as he usually did when he painted their portraits), she always went with him. He guarded her very closely, and very few people knew what she looked like, though the young men used to talk about her face and her singing. If she had Titian's blood in her veins, that would account for her marvellous skill at all embroidery. Somewhere in the middle of the century her godfather went to the Palace of the Closed Window to paint its master. It was then lived in by two brothers, Vitale and Giulio Civran. They were as proud as anybody in those times. Vitale was married, and had children. Young Giulio was still a wild fellow about town. While Titian was at work on Vitale's portrait, Margaret used to sit by him with her embroidery; and so you can see how it went. Vitale looked at her day after day, and determined to make her his. He became very gracious; none could be more so. The maestro, he said, painted too well to dine alone; would he not sit at the family board? The maestro never crossed the wills of his noble hosts if he could help it, and so now he made one of the company, with the family chaplain. The chaplain should never have taken orders. He had known a young man's life in Venice too, and was too great a friend of Giulio's to have any influence over him. But Giulio told him all his secrets; and that was how, when Margaret did not come to table with her godfather, that the young priest knew why. She was afraid to meet her lover Giulio in company. Vitale was much too cunning to allude to her, but he managed to meet her several times, and it maddened him to find that he could not make any impression upon her heart. His suits did not often fail, so he began to think. Of late he had remarked that his brother Giulio had become wonderfully well-behaved. Instead of disappearing for several days at a time, he was most domestic. The chaplain was very glad, for he thought Margaret a meet wife for any man.

"But one night Vitale crept up a little staircase and listened. He heard soft music in Margaret's room, and softer voices, and laughter. He ground his teeth, and came near bursting in. Then he heard the lovers talk. Margaret was being comforted for her fears. She told Giulio that their happiness could not last. Giulio swore it should last as long as their lives. But her heart trembled for his safety. Vitale terrified her, she said. Her eye had seen his evil look while he sat for his portrait. Vitale, standing in the dark staircase, heard them pour out their hearts to each other, and in Giulio's arms Margaret forgot her terrors. This was their plan. The next night Giulio was to go out on a pretended carousal, and come back at twelve. The chaplain was to be smuggled into her room by the little staircase. They were to be married, and fly for a time, till Titian's wrath should cool when he saw what a good husband Giulio made for his ward.

"Vitale had heard enough. He went to his friend Pomponio, and told him that Titian was playing a game in his household. A young gallant paid nightly visits to Margaret. This stung Pomponio to the quick. The idea of his father's double hypocrisy in keeping him away from his child and compassing her ruin himself, drove him wild. Vitale (who knew that Pomponio was Margaret's father) played well upon his feelings, and together they hatched a model plan. The chaplain was to be got rid of; Pomponio was to be admitted to his room and pass for him. 'I cannot permit a scandal like this to be in my house,' said Vitale. 'And your name must be shielded from such a family stain. You shall accompany me into Margaret's chamber, and you shall make them man and wife. I choose you to do this instead of the chaplain, so that the matter shall be known to no outsiders.' Vitale was clever enough to make Pomponio think that he and his brother Giulio were acting in concert. 'Giulio will summon you about midnight,' he said. 'We will arrange the rest upstairs. Keep your face concealed.'

"The next dusk came, and Vitale paid his chaplain a visit. He invited him to walk into the chapel. 'I am thinking of improving it,' he said. 'The Church will be well pleased with such devotion from your family,' answered the chaplain, wondering a little. 'See,' continued Vitale, 'this old chamber for vestments might go. It would make space, and a window could be put up in honor of our Saint Ambrose.' He unlocked the door with a key he held in his hand. The priest peered into the darkness, and pitched headlong thirty feet. Vitale laughed, and sent a prayer-book fluttering down after him. 'Read the marriage or the funeral service, whichever you prefer.' The bolt shot, and Vitale left the chapel.

"Meanwhile Giulio wandered about the city, waiting for the appointed time to come. He visited some of his old haunts, and was laughed at for his new soberness. At last he was at the chaplain's door. From the darkness of the room, Pomponio, who had been waiting, followed him out. They stepped noiselessly through the black halls and up the stairs. Giulio, in front, heard the stealthy tread of the priest behind him. Pomponio, as much a dupe as Giulio, in his turn, heard another step following in the dark below, and wondered what part whoever it was would be called on to play. Margaret met the two first at the door, and Pomponio marvelled that she showed no surprise at seeing that his companion was the younger Civran. 'Now begin, quick,' said the lover eagerly. Pomponio raised his face inquiringly. With a terrible oath at seeing him, Giulio wrenched out his sword. At the same instant Margaret shrieked and rushed into his arms; she had seen Vitale glide in. The sword pierced her body as Vitale's dagger plunged into his brother's shoulder up to the hilt. The main door burst open, and at it stood rooted the gray-bearded Titian, who had heard his girl's cry. She was dead; but Giulio, with an effort, wrenched himself round on the floor so that he saw Titian. 'Ah, it is a house of assassins, is it!' he exclaimed, and hurled his sword wildly at the appalled painter. It was the end. The weapon fell harmless midway, and Giulio rolled over by his bride's body. Pomponio wisely concealed himself from Titian. Giulio's death made it easy for Vitale to invent a plausible explanation of the affair to the old painter, whose heart was nearly broken. He sorrowed with the admirable Vitale over their common bereavement. Vitale secretly sent Pomponio to look after the chaplain, and Pomponio, seeing that he was dying, confessed to him his share in the plot. The chaplain died in a few hours, and Pomponio and Vitale kept their secret. Margaret lies here; but Giulio's body was never found."

The priest's story was finished, and its effect was to stun my reason. We all rose and went to the door. There I put some gold pieces into a box marked "For the restoration of the Church."

"I hope," I said, "that some of it may go to replacing the bust of the ill-starred Giulio by the side of his Margaret."

"It would be but an imaginary likeness, sir," murmured the priest.

"Something like this?" said Caspar suddenly. His pencil traced a rapid sketch of the portrait in the Louvre.

How shall I describe what happened? I heard an unearthly cry from the priest. A fierce wind flapped the curtains that hung over the entrance of the Cathedral, and we were all enveloped in their choking folds. When I extricated myself, Caspar and I were alone, and the stiletto was gone from my pocket.

The sun was near setting; we could stay here no longer. I searched for a moment among the crevices of the stone-work, but I knew such search was idle. We got into our gondola and started back. One phrase of Julian's had struck me with haunting significance. He had told us we should *remember him without the stiletto*. Our gondoliers sang at first as they rowed us along; soon, however, they grew as silent as ourselves. The night came down midway on our journey, and when we landed, the lights were twinkling in the water. Our train was to leave the next morning at half-past four. It was now too late for dinner at the hotel, so we got some food at a café. I do not remember that we spoke at all. If we said anything, it was of the most commonplace sort. We sat outside the café until it grew late. It hardly seemed possible to go to bed. We hailed a gondola, and had ourselves rowed idly about. Near the Ponte del Paradiso I felt my arm clutched.

"There he is!" said Caspar hoarsely.

I looked, and saw Julian walking slowly up the steps. I spoke to him, but he did not turn. He passed under the image of the Virgin into the narrow *calle*. Then I noticed a figure shadowing him, that came from I know not where.

"We must see about this," I said to Caspar.

We both landed, and entered the *calle*. The figures were some distance ahead, and we hastened our steps. We threaded our way through a maze of turns, and it seemed to me in the same direction we had once followed Julian before. The quarter changed from a deserted one to a place full of animation as we went farther into it. Lights gleamed, many figures passed to and fro, and strains of music filled the air. Julian ascended some steps, and we followed. This house was brilliant with light, and from the open upper windows came the thud and jingle of tambourines. One or two dominos flitted by us. We found ourselves at the doors of a wild fancy ball. The figures of men and women in rich costumes filled several rooms. Julian wore a very handsome dress himself. Several people spoke to him, and seemed to ask him to join the revels, but he walked quietly through the throng. At length a very pretty girl danced up to him laughing, and pulled him forward, but he smiled down on her and shook his head. Never have I seen a happier look on any man's face. Could Caspar have painted him as he was now, his fame would indeed have been secure. The girl put her arms as nearly round Julian's neck as she could, but he made no return of her caress. Then she left him with pouting lips, and joined a young fellow who seemed contented enough with his good-fortune. Another figure was speaking to Julian. The music had grown wilder, and the dance was whirling with spectral rapidity. I looked at the gaudily painted walls; they seemed oddly familiar. Could they bear any relation to the blistered remains of those old haunts Julian had shown us? I had no time to think of anything, for Julian now was leaving the hall. He descended into the street, and once more I saw the figure creep after him. For an instant I was near enough behind him to have been able to swear it was Julian's double, so like was his gait and build, though he seemed somehow like an older man. But I could not see his face. The walk began again. The pace increased, for Julian was hurrying with more speed at every turn. Lamps, doorways, black water, then walls again, all whizzed by. We had begun to run; but as Caspar and I did not know the ground, we stumbled here, made a wrong turn there, and found at length that the figures had utterly disappeared. We groped about for a moment, and found ourselves opposite a garden wall. A lamp revealed the Palace of the Closed Window looming above us. Then from an upper floor came a piercing scream; then nothing but the water lapping lazily against the stones. A violent grip was laid on my arm, and I saw Caspar's face, hideous with terror.

"Up — up there!" he gasped.

The space of the walled window was lambent with a vapory light. Caspar swayed and staggered so that I had to exert all my force to keep him from slipping into the water. Suddenly a dark mass filled part of the window. Something plunged through the air, and fell into the canal with a splash. My eyes for one instant saw Julian's face, ghastly with death, and then the water closed above him in turbulent eddies.

Over the heaving surface swept a black garment, and the young priest of Torcello passed close and melted into the night. By some inward flash of the mind it was revealed to me that it was the murdered chaplain who had talked with us by the tomb in that dim church corner.

When the good people at the Three Wise Men came to the spot at our instance, and heard what we had to say, they were of the opinion that our dinner at the café had put us in the humor for practical jokes. Nothing could persuade them to inform the police.

"Why, that is the Palace of the Closed Window, and the Signori tell us that they saw through a wall! Eh! body of Bacchus! the Signori are merry!" said they.

In three hours we had left Venice.

Some time ago I had a despondent letter from Caspar. He wrote that all creative talent in him seemed dead. He traced it to that morning when he had encountered Julian alone. The last accounts of him were, that he had given up his Weimar studio and gone to Paris, where I am told he has taken to making copies of the picture in the Louvre.

No one spoke for some time after Ralph had finished. The breeze had almost died away, and the "Hope's" sail flapped gently as she glided through the water whose ripples were full of phosphorescent gleams. Fleecy clouds veiled the moon, which had begun to wane, and had taken on to-night a reserved air of mystery, as if it had been for something in Ralph's story, and might have elucidated some dark points.

Presently Mrs. Chauncey said: "Well, Mr. Travers, your story is grewsome indeed. I am sure I shall not sleep to-night with dreaming of that dreadful Vitale and that fascinating Giulio and poor, dear Margaret. But why was the stiletto taken away? And why—"

"You mustn't ask me," said Ralph. "I have only told the story as it happened. You must ask the moon. See what a weird, mysterious smile she wears. She will tell you to-night, in those sleepless dreams of yours."

They made two boatloads from the yacht to the landing. Ralph and Mrs. Chauncey and Mr. and Mrs. Bowdoin went off first, and when the gig came back the rest got into it, and Charlie

Wyatt went with them. As he took Muriel's hand to help her out of the boat, he said, "Remember, my light burns always for you. Ah, if I could only think you looked out of your window sometimes, and gave one kind thought to the poor fellow who lies awake hour after hour, and paces the deck in the night-watches thinking of you!"

"Hush, hush!" was Muriel's only reply.

"Good-night!" "Good-night!" sounded in the air from many voices.

Charlie Wyatt's manly tones shouted, "Attention! Dip oars! Give way!" and the boat shot silently and quickly out of the harbor.

When Muriel stood at her window an hour or two later, it was very dark outside. The wind had risen, and the waters sounded angry and threatening. The "Hope's" light burned on, — the only spot of light to be seen, — and by its gleam the vessel seemed to be pitching and tossing as if impatient at being held fast; "frenetic to be free." Muriel turned from the window. Were there tears in her eyes?

The hour which might have been, yet might not be.
                      . . . on what shore
Bides it the breaking of Time's weary sea?
                    DANTE GABRIEL ROSSETTI.

But only the one Hope's one name be there,
Not less nor more, but even that word alone.
                                        IBID.

FIFTH DAY.

It had rained in the night, but the day dawned brilliantly.

"We shall hear Bell's story by the big oak-tree," said Mrs. Temple. "We will carry camp-chairs and shawls and rugs."

"You will all get wet driving through the woods; I warn you to wear waterproof garments," said Mr. Bowdoin. "Margaret will probably tell you no one takes cold by being wet at Fair Harbor. I believe she thinks the rain is mixed with Jamaica ginger and hot-drops. Nevertheless, I advise wraps."

"By the way," said Mrs. Chauncey, "what did Mrs. Nye mean the other day by saying there were more 'waterers' here than usual this fall? I haven't seen a water-cart since I came."

The others laughed heartily, and Ralph said: "It is a local expression, Mrs. Chauncey, and reminds me of a conversation I heard early this morning between Jim Canaan and Miss Carr-Wynstede's maid, which will answer your question. I was in the stable, and they were standing just outside, Marie gathering lemon-balm to make 'tisane de mélisse,' she told me. I shall dramatize the conversation: —

Jim. Won't you come out for a bit of a sail, Miss Maree? [By the bye, you know he has christened his catamaran the "Maree"!]

Marie. I have fear; it makes much wind to-day.

Jim. Not a bit of it. It's just a good little breeze that'll send the boat hummin'. You ain't like them waterers that calls a cupful of wind a squall.

Marie. What is it a waterer, and what is it a squall? I know them not.

Jim. Well, a waterer is a party from the city that comes down here to stop, and they mostly begins by sayin' they likes sailin' better 'n anything, and then you take 'em out in the little harbor here, where you can sail a child's boat, and they screeches and wants to land before they gets out into deep water, and talks about squalls and storms and bein' seasick. That's a waterer. And a squall — well, a squall's half a gale.

Marie. Ah, I see. Well, as you say I am not like a waterer, and you are sure there will be no tempest, I will go. Mademoiselle said I might."

"She did go," said Muriel, "and came back in a fine flush of excitement and sunburn. I don't know about that attractive ' homme aux homards!' I should like to take Marie home with me."

The Professor came just then to claim Muriel's promise to walk to Wood's Holl with him. He was going to see his friend Professor B——d, of the Fish Commission, and he wanted to show Muriel the Government Buildings there, and present to her the amiable gentleman who presided over the wonders of the deep.

"What a charming creature that English girl is, to be sure!" exclaimed Mrs. Chauncey. "What a pity she isn't an American! She doesn't seem to be a bit like the others, — ' Lady

Barberina,' for instance; for I always think of her as a real person."

"No, she is not in the least like Lady Barberina," said Mrs. Bowdoin, "and yet — she is not like us. It is such folly to talk about our being cousins, and coming from the same stock, and all that. We are as different from them as possible; in education, in tastes, in ideas, in manners, — every way. In England, where I was constantly told about blood being stronger than water, and how, after all, we *ought* to feel at home there, and what sympathy should exist between two nations, one the child of the other, — the same speech, same religion, and all the rest, — I generally assented, for of course it was meant as a compliment, and Americans don't like to seem rude. English people don't mind it, and so perhaps speak more truths than we. But once I burst out before an innocent British female who was going on in that strain, and almost astonished her to death by saying, 'No, no! it is no such thing! We are not at all like you. We don't dress like you' (Heaven forbid!), 'nor speak like you' (the more's the pity!), 'nor look nor think nor act nor love nor hate like you. For myself, I am at home in France with French people, and in Italy with the Italians; not in England with the English.' The good lady opened her eyes, and answered never a word. But I spoke the truth."

"I must confess," said Mrs. Chauncey, "that in the matter of dress they have immensely improved of late years. Some of the really nicest people dress very well. Sometimes I am afraid they make American women look as if they were a little over-dressed, — as if Worth and the rest had been too much for them, — and when Englishwomen do have good figures, they are uncommonly good. I cannot understand why they should have such beautiful long throats and long limbs, just because long throats and limbs are the fashion, brought in by Burne Jones and those sub-Raphaelite folks. In a Redfern-cut dress and jacket, fitting as the English tailors alone do fit, I make them my best bow, compelled by a sense of justice, not because I care to bow to them, Heaven knows. You 'd better never bow to an Englishwoman first, if you can help it; as a rule, if you let them alone and look the other way, you'll find them saluting you."

"Have you ever noticed one curious thing about English people?" asked Margaret. "They call everybody 'foreigners' but themselves, no matter where they may happen to be. Once in Rome an English lady said to me, 'I see you pass much of your time with foreigners here! Do you like foreigners?' 'What do you mean?' said I; 'whom do you call foreigners? English? Americans? Russians?' 'Oh no,' she replied, 'I meant Romans. I see you so much with Romans!' She really seemed to think that Romans were the 'foresticri' on their own soil, and she the native inhabitant and proprietor. It is very amusing."

"Kirkland seems to have been a good deal disgusted in England and on the Continent," said Ralph, "with the silly, undignified way in which American girls, and still worse, American mothers, behave with regard to society. It has been the fashion lately, especially among the English, to 'take up' Americans, as they call it. The very phrase is offensive. We, who see in our American women everything that is most charming, are at first disposed to think it quite natural that they should be noticed and admired. And looked at in one light, it is all very nice and flattering. But, by Jove! it makes my blood boil to see and hear the sort of thing that goes on sometimes. The 'certain condescension in foreigners,' that Lowell writes about, tinges a great deal of the attention our country men and women receive, and makes a sensitive person wince and want to kick somebody. We all know that there is nothing an English husband or brother of decent pride likes *less* than that his wife or sister should be made conspicuous by the smiles and favor of a certain high personage, whose smiles and favors are too promiscuous and too compromising to be desirable; yet I have seen lovely American cheeks flush and eyes glisten, and have almost heard hearts beat with excitement and pleasure, if only those royal eyes turned upon them; and if he asked to have them presented, and — oh, joy of joys! — if he took them out in the waltz, or in to supper on his august arm, their cup of happiness overflowed. And the blackguards they marry, to be called My Lady, and to belong to his Royal Highness's set! It is unbelievable!"

"If American girls choose to transplant themselves, and marry Englishmen for titles and position, giving *their* handfuls of silver for the ribbon on their lords' coats, or their place in Debrett, it is their own affair; but that an American man should take to himself an English wife, and run the risk of enduring, like Lady Barberina's husband, an ignominious exile, or else of keeping his wife over here bound to be unhappy and forever homesick, seems to me little short of madness."

All this Mrs. Bowdoin uttered quite fast and rather irrelevantly, standing outside the window as she spoke, and apparently addressing Polly.

"That's so! That's so!" shouted Polly, who was in great spirits to-day.

Nobody knew Ralph's opinion on this point, for he seemed to be suddenly needed in the stable, as he marched off in that direction.

"I meant every word of that, Polly," said

Mrs. Bowdoin gravely. And Polly mumbled something which savored of approval.

"We had better start for the tree betimes after lunch, don't you think?" said Margaret. "I thought we would make no pretence of a picnic to-day. It is so much more comfortable to get home in time to dress for dinner, and eat it nicely at a table like Christians."

Muriel and the Professor came back just before luncheon, the Professor bearing a tin pail filled with water in which was a beautiful "Portuguese man-of-war," which one of the men had brought in while they were at the Fish Commission.

"And yet they laugh about the Gulf Stream," said Margaret. "Wait till you see the Spanish mackerel I have for your dinner, and see if you think they would be better in Florida!"

They had at last arranged themselves under the oak-tree. Some were in riding-habits, and some had driven. Bell had the seat of honor, with her back to the tree, in the Scheveningen chair (a wagonful of chairs and cushions having been sent on before them), and the others grouped themselves in front of her.

"I am a good deal agitated," she said. "The branches really hit hard and hurt me as we drove through the woods, and I was soaked with water. Give me the very thickest of those rugs, please, Tom. It is extremely damp on the ground. How can you lose all sense of truth as you do here, Margaret? It is very sad. You are like an 'enfant du midi,' when it comes to the Cape. Do you remember what Daudet says of the 'enfant du midi' in that most deliciously witty book, 'Tartarin de Tarascon'? 'L'homme du midi ne ment pas ; il se trompe. Il ne dit pas toujours la vérité, mais il croit le dire. Son mensonge à lui, ce n'est pas le mensonge, c'est le mirage.' With Margaret, Gulf Stream stands for 'mirage.'"

"Now, having basely accused your best and only sister of falsehood," said Margaret, laughing, "where is your story?"

"Here it is," said Bell, producing it from the folds of her wrap. "It looks to be rather a bulky manuscript, but somehow or other I could n't stop. I intended to keep to a dry statement of some facts that were told to me a few years ago, but I found my pencil running away with me. I fancy it's also an effect of the Gulf Stream; it weakens one's character. I have heard too that diffuseness is a fault of young authors."

"It's a trifle hard on their readers sometimes," said Tom quietly.

"How sorry you would be if you were made to go out in that punt and fish for pickerel, and so lose the hearing of it!" his wife answered seriously; and then, as he looked repentant, she began.

IN WAR-TIME;

OR, ONLY A WOMAN'S SHOE.

In the autumn of 1870, when poor France was reading the last pages of her record of insufficiency and defeat, it so happened that a regiment of Uhlans was quartered in the little French town of ——. It would be of no purpose were I to tell the name of the town, or, indeed, of the regiment, as a bit of mystery is always best when a story is half true. Naturally the officers of this regiment were put into the most comfortable quarters that the place afforded, and were scattered about in the outlying châteaux that nestled among the low, wooded hills surrounding the town. A captain and two lieutenants were sent to the Château d'Autancy (here I must give the name), and on the morning before their arrival a polite note from the colonel of the regiment announced their coming to the family. This family was, alas! very small now, for the father and mother were dead, and the only brother was shut up in Paris, wounded. So Claire, his sister, and an elderly maiden aunt who had lived with them since the death of the parents were alone at the château.

As my story begins, the two ladies were sitting round a pleasant wood-fire in the cheerless little salon, which in the former and grander days had been used as an insignificant morning-room, but now, in the dwindled state of the family, served as sitting-room and music-room, morning and evening room, all in one. The large envelope, sealed with portentous red wax, was brought in by the old butler, who peered at it with the greatest curiosity. Claire d'Autancy, to whom it was addressed, opened it with some trepidation, and then turned to her aunt, her cheeks scarlet with indignation.

"See what shame is put upon us," she cried, "by those dogs of Prussians!"

"Give it to me, my dear," said Mademoiselle de Varenne; and putting on her glasses she read that the high and well-born Otto von Barheim, captain of the —th Uhlans, and the high and well-born lieutenants von Aarburg and von Sonnstein, with servants and horses, would be quartered at the Château d'Autancy, from the coming morrow until further orders from the General of Division.

"Well, dear child, we must submit; and I only hope that the manners of these barbarians will not be too shocking. We must never see them if we can help it, — you especially, Claire." And she drew herself up as stiffly as her embonpoint would permit, and tried to look stern, which was impossible.

"But, Tante, I don't see how we can avoid meeting them," said poor Claire. "I hate them, these Prussians; but we must eat, and really Babette cannot cook as if for a hotel. We must all dine together, I suppose, bad as it will be. We need not converse, you know. But how horrible, how humiliating it all is!"

"Ah, child, it is the fortune of war! We must be polite, but patriotic. It may happen that we can be of the greatest service to our dear country."

"How do you mean, Tante? Shall we poison these creatures?"

"Do not jest, my Claire. Wait only, and we shall see, — we shall see. I will now give my mind to it, and come to some conclusion."

Aunt Artémise's conclusions were generally arrived at by the aid of, and in company with, innumerable works of fiction, the perusal of which was her daily occupation and delight. The elder Dumas furnished her with history, romance, and adventure. She was apt to return to him after excursions in more modern and realistic fields, saying, "Get me a volume of my favorite, Claire; I get amusement from him, and can believe his facts or not, as I choose. I don't have to think too much about it, which is a comfort; and I am not shocked, which is a gain."

Her habit was to have her morning cup of chocolate in bed, her novel in hand; not to hurry after that, but manage to be dressed and take a stroll in the garden before the twelve o'clock déjeuner. And, if the truth were told, she was very apt to put on a loose gown and recline on the broad couch in her chamber, to read in quiet, as she said; and she would not usually be seen again until sunset in summer, or twilight in winter, when she would walk on the terrace in her gray satin dinner-dress, to get an appetite for that late meal. She did not care to drive: why should she, she asked. She knew all the roads, and Heaven knew that the country was not amusing. So Claire had a lonely life of it, especially now, in war-time, when the châteaux in the neighborhood were nearly all shut up and deserted.

The next morning there was a great clattering in the courtyard which enclosed the farm-buildings and stables. There were many empty stalls, alas! as the fortunes of the family were not as flourishing as in the old time, and Gaston had taken two horses with him to the war. Claire had to make a bargain between her patriotism and her curiosity, in order to allow herself to look from a shaded window to see what manner of brutes these were that had come to take possession. Of the three men, — gentlemen, as she reluctantly confessed to her patriotism, — the oldest looked about thirty, and brown with war and weather. The other two seemed quite young, one a mere boy, with open blue eyes and a very incipient moustache. She could not help thinking of his mother and sister in far-off Germany, and their anxiety for this lad. "Well, they never should have come," her patriotism answered her. As soon as the luggage — not much to speak of — had arrived and been put in the rooms assigned to the invaders, they all clattered off again to headquarters, and Claire and Tante were left to their breakfast, with no interruption. But before dinner they returned, and when that repast was served the two ladies had to meet their conquerors. This was done in silence, and with great dignity and ceremony, the ladies making slight and cold obeisance, courtesying with averted face, and the officers bringing their heels together simultaneously with a loud click, and bowing at the same moment, like figures on a hand-organ. It was not a gay dinner. Old Antoine looked as if he wished that each morsel might choke the Germans, as indeed he did. There were a few constrained remarks by Von Barheim, the older officer, in grammatical French and a bad accent, and as many monosyllabic replies from Tante Artémise. Claire scarcely raised her long lashes, and wished that she had not so good an appetite; but she could not really scorn the food partaken of by such distasteful guests, for she was a healthy girl of nineteen, living a life in the open air, and, in truth, she *had to eat.* After dinner more courtesies, more clicking of heels, and all intercourse was over for that day.

"Well, dear child, it was not so impossibly bad after all," said Tante, as they sipped their coffee in the little salon.

"I think it was bad," cried Claire, "and the stiffness and silence were horrible; I know that youngest one thought so, for I caught him giggling to himself,

and the Captain looked at him sternly, quite sternly;
but I am sure I felt like laughing myself, just because
I wanted to cry. How long will this last?"

"Claire, I have thought of something as I was reading the 'Three Guardsmen' to-day. We must intercept their letters."

"Must do *what*, Tante?"

Aunt Artémise glowed all over with satisfaction, and her silver-gray barrel curls quite trembled as she disclosed her plan. What more natural than that Antoine should say to the Captain that all letters could be put on the old oak chest in the gallery, — the chest just outside the door of the apartment given to the Prussians? Then at night, after all was quiet, Claire and she would obtain possession of their dangerous documents, — for of course they would be dangerous.

"We must not leave it for servants to do, my dearest; they must all be able to be innocent when questioned. No, to us must belong the glory, but also the danger. If, on reading these letters, we find mischief, we will manage to send them to Paris somehow, perhaps by balloon; but at any rate we can prevent their reaching their destination." And the worthy lady leaned back in her chair, exhausted by her noble enthusiasm.

"Oh, dear Tante, what a delightful plan!" said

Claire, her eyes sparkling. "We will manage it, never fear. Can't we begin this very night?"

So Antoine was told to say his message to Captain von Barheim, which he did, in innocence of any dark treason. I must explain a bit the situation of this "gallery library" and its connection with the rest of the house. It was a long, narrow room, running at the back of the old state apartments, which were in the story above the hall, dining-room, and so forth, and were never used now. It connected the two wings of the château, and was a sort of nondescript place, delightful in its way. On one side of it were shelves reaching almost to the ceiling, full of books, manuscripts, and pamphlets, which had been tucked into corners as the years went on. On the other side were windows — old mullioned windows with deep seats — whence one could look out over the peaceful country, with carefully kept orchards and cultivated fields, with woods on the low hill-tops, and the spires of the little town two miles or so away. One of the windows opened on to a small porch, and steps with a quaint balustrade of old iron led into the courtyard below. So it was called the gallery library, and Claire had passed many pleasant hours there, from the time when her little feet first pattered and stumbled over its floor, paved with small red bricks.

I will not give you an exact account of how they obtained possession of the first letters left on the old oak chest near the door of the gallery leading into the " Prussian apartment," as it was now to be called. Suffice it to say that at the dark time before dawn the two were in Tante Artémise's chamber, eagerly bending over their booty, before them on the table. There was only one letter, addressed in a bold handwriting to " Baron von Altenstein, Frankfurt am Main." " That is just our affair," said Tante in a loud stage whisper.

Claire felt strangely averse to breaking the seal, considering that it was an heroic act ; but conquering her hesitation she tore open the envelope. As she did it, she said, —

" But, Tante, we can't read that horrid German handwriting ; why were we so stupid as not to think of that? But stay, we are in luck ; it is in French ! "

And in French it was ; the writer beginning his epistle by saying that as all officers were enjoined to learn and diligently practise the French tongue, he found it best to write his letters in that language, it being pleasanter than any other kind of exercise. There was lamentably little of political importance, — nothing, indeed. It was a simple, friendly letter, saying that he had the good fortune to be quartered in a charming old château. " For the sake of the inmates," it went on to say, "I hope our stay here may be short. It cannot be pleasant for them, though I shall do my best to make it peaceful, keeping the servants to quiet ways and early hours, and the two youngsters busy with carrying unimportant despatches to the colonel in the town. How is the fair Hildegarde? Are her eyes as blue and as serious as ever? By the way, did you ever happen to see blue eyes with black hair? It is rather an attractive combination;" and with a little more the letter ended.

They looked rather blankly at each other. "Better luck next time, dear child."

"Perhaps so, Tante;" and the young girl tore the paper into small pieces, and threw them angrily into the fire. "Good-night," she said, and went to her room.

Claire passed a feverish and unrefreshing night, and when she got up in the morning she felt nervous and unsatisfied. She wandered out into the garden quite early, and betook herself to a little pavilion which was at the end of a long straight path bordered on either side with high box hedges. This little summer-house was a favorite resort of Claire's. It had no special beauty of situation, and one only saw from it the smiling cultivated valley, the long quiet slopes of which always seemed to possess a certain essence of afternoon; but she liked it, and I think it soothed her somewhat impatient and untried spirit, — this mellow aspect of field and sky. She liked to think that perhaps far over the faint blue line of the low hills, away there near the sky, her fate might be waiting for her, and that if she might only reach their summit and look beyond, she would see a fair new life lying there before her. As she sat dreaming, she heard a foot on the gravel-path, — a booted and spurred foot, — and she shrank back into her retreat. Captain von Barheim strode leisurely past her, went to the edge of the terraced garden, and stood looking out over the valley, so that she could see his face. It was a manly, honest face, as she was forced to acknowledge to herself, and a sad one, as he gazed out into the distance, evidently seeing not this French land, but a far different country, over hill and dale and river.

"Perhaps he is thinking of that Hildegarde he writes of," she said to herself, and then colored angrily that she should remember that there was a Hildegarde. She wished much to get away unperceived, and moved a little; but he heard her and turned. She must have made a very pretty picture as she sat there within the low doorway, framed in vine-leaves yellow with autumn. I fancy he thought so, for he started, and went toward her.

"Good-morning, Mademoiselle."

"Good-morning," she said, and rose to go.

"Stay one moment, Mademoiselle, and let me say to you what I feel so deeply. It annoys me beyond expression that I and my companions should be obliged to trouble you with our presence. The intrusion should not last another day, another hour, if I had any power to put an end to it."

"You cannot dislike to be here as much as I dislike to have you!" cried poor Claire, forgetting her manners. "But after all, it might have been just the other way. My brother might have been in Germany with our army, quartered in one of your quiet homes; it only happened so!"

"Yes, it only happened so," he said quietly, but biting his long moustache to hide the smile that would come. "And if your brother had been quartered in one of our quiet homes, I hope that some fair Châtelaine would have shown him the courtesy which I have had given me here. It is exile, after all, you know, Mademoiselle, and not all a gay fanfaron of trumpets. And we have our dead to think of as well as our absent ones, — comrades who will not return with us when we go."

Somehow Claire had not taken that view of the matter, and it suddenly struck her that his people at home must be anxious, that that Hildegarde was *very* anxious perhaps, and she felt a pang of remorse and pity. She looked at him with something of all this in her eyes, so that he read the softened glance, and said, —

"Then you will be a little sorry for me, although you hate me?"

"Yes;" and making him a little gesture of farewell, she turned and went quickly away up the garden path.

Much to Aunt Artémise's discomfiture, Claire refused to have anything to do with looking for letters that night, and indeed for many nights. When pressed, she made excuses for not doing a patriot's duty, and all things went on quietly. Indeed, the days would have seemed rather empty and dull now, without the coming and going of horses and men, and the little element of uncertainty which lent variety to the hours. The meetings at meals gradually lost a little of their rigid and cold ceremony, and took on a more bearable aspect. Tante's kind heart melted more than she at all liked, at the uniformly polite and pleasant bearing of those hated conquerors; but she made spasmodic efforts to be stern.

One day at déjeuner there were some very fine pears on the table. Tante Artémise looked at them and said to Antoine, "Where did those pears come from? Our trees bear none so handsome." Antoine hesitated, and Von Barheim answered for him.

"I saw them as I was taking a long ride this morning, Mademoiselle, and ventured to bring a basketful back with me, thinking that they might be sweet and good. I hope you will find them so."

Tante Artémise looked very indignant, and when Antoine handed the fruit to her, said, "Merci, no! Our poor peasants cannot defend their orchards, it seems!"

Von Barheim colored angrily, and cried, "I can assure you, Mademoiselle de Varennes, that they were well paid for!" And then he added more gently, "The poor old woman seemed very glad to sell them."

There was a pause. Artémise looked very uncomfortable, but evidently thought it impossible to apologize to an enemy, and the young lieutenants stared at the patterns on their plates, lest their eyes should meet, and they be betrayed into unseemly mirth. Then Claire's voice was heard, low but very distinct, —

"Antoine, give me the pears, if you please;" and taking one, she tasted it, and said to Von Barheim, "It is delicious, Monsieur."

He thanked her with a smile full of gratitude, and harmony was restored.

One afternoon Tante Artémise went to the gallery library to get the third volume of "Ange Pitou," when, looking casually towards the oak chest where the letters were put, she saw one, which she incontinently seized and brought in triumph away.

When Claire came upstairs to dress for dinner, she called her into the little boudoir between their two chambers and begged her to open it, as it was addressed to Captain von Barheim. Claire looked anything but eager, but at last took it and opened it, and after one glance cried pettishly, "There, Tante, you see how useless and silly all this is! It is in German handwriting, and would do us no good if it contained the whole plan of a campaign!"

"Well, well, dear, at least we can burn it, so that it shall do the enemy no good;" and taking it from Claire, she put it in the fire.

"Tante," pleaded poor Claire, "I really don't see that we are doing our country any service, and I cannot but think that we are wrong."

"Wrong, you child without a patriot soul!" answered Artémise, ruffling with disdain. "Do you not know that many of the greatest acts in history have been accomplished by the aid of intercepted letters?

Let me see," — and she began to search her memory for instances in the pages of her dear Dumas.

"No matter," interrupted Claire, a little frightened at the thought of the mass of evidence about to be brought against her; "perhaps it is all right, but I don't like to do it."

"The highest duties are sometimes the most painful," asserted Tante, still in her severest tone ; " and this very night I wish you to join me in trying to find this dangerous correspondence which is going on under our very roof, — for of course it must be going on, — and I shall consider you as wanting in all the spirit of your ancestors if you fail me now !"

"Not to-night, dear Tante, but to-morrow night," said Claire, feeling a very traitor to the spirit of her ancestors ; and there the matter rested.

At dinner she scarcely dared to look at poor Von Barheim, feeling quite bewildered and unhappy. He, on the other hand, was more than usually agreeable, making his best effort to talk of things with no bearing on wars or rumors of wars. When she went to her chamber, she sat for a long time brushing her hair and dreamily looking at herself in the glass. At last she leaned her chin upon her two hands and examined with some interest the color of her eyes. "Yes, they certainly are quite, quite blue, and my hair is black.

So that is an attractive combination, is it?" Then she was angry, and said "Nonsense!" to herself in the glass, and went to bed.

The next morning Claire went off for a long walk, and was on her way back, thinking that she might be a little late for the déjeuner, when in a hedged lane outside of her own domain she met a rough-looking fellow in a tattered blouse, who stopped, as if to let her pass; she looked up, supposing him to be some one of the peasants who knew her, and had her customary pleasant greeting on her lips, when she saw that he was a stranger. He said he was hungry and wanted some money to buy a dinner.

"I have no money, my good man, but come to the château and they shall give you a good bowl of soup," she answered, not frightened; for although he had an insolent manner, yet he was a Frenchman, and probably lived not very far from her neighborhood.

"None of your soup for me, my pretty demoiselle; I want something stronger. Here, give me those earrings out of your dainty ears, and I will go; but if not, I shall take them, and a kiss into the bargain," and he laughed coarsely.

Claire was thoroughly alarmed now, but she could not bear the thought of giving up her little pearl earrings, which had been her mother's; she looked up and down the lane, but all was empty and silent, and she was just taking the trinkets from her ears with trembling fingers, when she heard the sound of a horse's hoofs, and turning again saw through the vista made by the overarching branches of the high thornbushes a horseman coming quickly. She waved her hand and ran a few steps toward him, and before she was quite conscious of what happened, the peasant had disappeared through a hole in the hedge, and Von Barheim was at her side, and off his horse in a moment.

"What is it? Are you hurt?" and he looked pale and agitated.

"No, no, but the fellow was very rude, and if you had not come, I should have had to give up my earrings;" and she held out one in her hand as she spoke.

"Where did he go?" And he was on his horse again.

"Oh, pray don't! There may be more of them!" and she trembled and looked so frightened that he dismounted and gave up all idea of chasing the criminal. They walked slowly side by side, his well-trained horse following just behind.

"You should never walk alone outside of your own grounds," he said quite sternly. "Don't you know that it cannot be safe in a time like this?"

"But I have always done it, and forgot that it would be different now. All the people in the country round know me, and are respectful and kind."

"This, then, was one of our camp stragglers? It shall be looked into, and I think we shall catch the fellow before night."

"No, no! Indeed—in fact— It was not a German," she stammered at last, with such a pitiful glance at having to make the confession, that he laughed; and then she laughed, and they strolled amicably back to the château, talking of other things. When they reached the little gate that opened into the park, he said, —

"Now promise me, Mademoiselle, that you will not walk beyond your own limits, unless, indeed, you allow me to accompany you," he added smiling.

"But that could not be, you know," answered Claire seriously; and he was silent. They separated on the terrace. She held out her hand quietly, and said, "Thank you," and he bowed his head gravely over it, saying, —

"It was nothing, Mademoiselle."

I need not say how mean and guilty Claire felt, when Tante reminded her that evening that she had promised to go letter-hunting in the night. But there was nothing left to her but to keep her word, and indeed she feared that if she refused again, Artémise would begin to suspect something of the strange tumult in her young heart and brain. She sat by the smouldering embers of the fire in her chamber, in her long white loose gown, until after midnight, when she went and knocked at Tante's door and said she was ready.

"How white you look!" said that worthy conspirator.

It certainly could not be said of her, for she was clad in a strange garment of crimson woollen stuff, falling full from a yoke, which made her look like a very old baby, that resemblance being heightened by a very be-ruffled lace cap, with lappets. They proceeded with great caution to the door which opened from their part of the house into the gallery library, and went in. A lantern on a post in the courtyard was always kept lighted at night, and shone dimly through the deep windows, making it quite possible to find one's way, and even to discern objects. As they walked on tiptoe toward the farther end of the long room Artémise whispered anxiously,—

"Child of my soul, thou hast on thy *mules*, and they click loudly on the pavement; take them off, or thou losest us!"

Claire stooped, took off the offending slippers, and holding them in one hand went swiftly on to the oak chest; there she saw a white envelope, clutched it, and turned to go back. Tante trotted nimbly on before her, and they had already accomplished three quarters of their way, when an ominous noise was heard,—a sound from the other side of the Prussian door; the handle grated as it was turned. Their retreat now became a rout. Tante, though stout, could be quite agile when occasion demanded, and being considerably in advance of Claire, reached their door in safety. Claire made desperate haste, and when she neared the threshold, gave a leap into the passage beyond, dropping one shoe in her effort, but holding fast the letter.

Von Barheim had sat in his room rather later than usual, first writing, and then by the fire, musing on many things. He was roused from his thoughts by a slight sound in the gallery, which was only separated from his chamber by a small anteroom, the door of which was open. Yes, there was certainly something or somebody moving out there with a little click-clack on the brick floor. Then it stopped, and he thought it must have been a mouse, when again, nearer the door, he distinguished a soft rustle and motion. He remembered the window opening to the courtyard, and bethinking himself that the country was infested by tramps, as always in war-time, he went quietly to the table where he had laid his sword, and then crossed the anteroom and opened the door. What did he see? No tramp with burglarious intent, but at the end of the gallery a white and youthful figure, the light full upon it from the window near, rushing out at the door, with great floating of garments. He stood for a moment undecided, then going back for a candle, walked to the end of the long room. What was that on the floor? He picked it up, and turned it round and round in his hand as if it were some curious toy. It was a very small blue silk *mule*, a perfectly French shoe, with a high heel, but cut away from the sides and back of the foot; in fact, like the watch-pockets sold at fairs to hang up at the side of one's bed. Silly shoes, perhaps, with only a toe and a sole and a heel, but very pretty and comfortable withal to slip one's feet into; not meant, however, for such warlike advance and retreat as the present. He went slowly back to his room, still looking at the shoe with a curiously pleased and tender light in his honest eyes. As he passed the oak chest on which he had put a letter not an hour before, he saw that there was no letter there. Had it fallen to the floor? A careful search convinced him that such was not the case. Then he looked at the shoe again, and it suddenly flashed into his somewhat slow Teutonic brain that they belonged to each other, had some connection,—this small slipper and his letter. He went into his room, sat down again by his fire, and fell to thinking anew, still holding the slipper in his hand.

Meantime the two ladies had reached their apartment, and going into Tante Artémise's chamber, sank exhausted,—Claire on a low chair by the fire, and Tante at full length on her couch, panting, and as red as her gown.

"My treasure, we are safe!" she gasped. "What an escape, what a *coup de théâtre!* Where is the letter for which we have risked so much? I hope it will repay our devotion to our dear country!"

Claire did not seem to think that it would, as she held up one foot in a pink silk stocking to the fire, rather piteously.

"I have lost one of my *mules*," she said. "I think I must have dropped it in the gallery."

"Ah, well, child, that is nothing. Marrette can find it for you in the morning. Now for the letter!"

Claire opened the envelope, which was addressed to the same Von Altenstein as the former one. She did it with the greatest inward repugnance, and, indeed, read with so much hesitation that Tante reproached her more than once for her want of spirit. It was written in the most intimate tone, saying that the writer was beginning to get a little anxious at the non-arrival of any word from his friend.

"We burned that one, I suppose, my dear," interrupted Tante Artémise.

"We are in daily and hourly expectation of orders to move," it went on.

"Ah, Claire, now at last we shall find something of importance;" and she sat upright on her couch, stiff with interest. "We shall unmask the enemy's movements. We shall be of the greatest service, and we shall win renown."

"Wait, Tante," said Claire languidly. "I do not think with you."

And indeed that was all of the matter that was hinted at. Von Barheim wrote in rather a sad mood, saying that he felt restless and unsatisfied:—

"Ah, my Carl, how terrible a thing is war! How the nations sit and watch each other, greedy to snatch a bit of territory, and jealous to defend some fancied right! This horrible feeling of national hatred may so often have broken apart two lives which might have grown together and been happy. I fear I am losing something of my manly impulse, for I find myself wondering in this peaceful château — peaceful except that I disturb its quiet — whether this national glory of Vaterland be worth all the suffering it brings, and whether a nation could not be more glorious by peace than by war! But you will laugh at me, my Carl, and perhaps you would be right; still, it relieves me of my dull mood to put a little of its weight upon your heart. Good-by, trusty friend and comrade. God grant that we meet before long!

"MAX VON BARHEIM."

As Claire read on to the end, she forgot Tante, she forgot all but the words before her. She read slowly and thoughtfully, more as if she were listening than speaking. When she finished, she looked up with a start, as if coming back to the situation. Then she cried, —

"Tante, this is the last time I will do this thing! I hate it! Remember, I will never do it again!" and the tears rushed to her eyes.

"Softly, softly, child; we will see. To be sure, I am rather disappointed not to have found anything of consequence. I did not quite understand all that about peace and war; it seemed a strange letter for a Prussian."

Claire made no answer, but put the letter quietly, almost reverently, into the fire, and watched it smoke, and burst into flame for a moment, and then settle into a little gray, quivering ghost of itself, until it floated up the chimney as if to seek its own way to its far-off destination. Then she went to her own room without a word and shut the door.

The next morning she did not go out as usual, but sat by her window until she saw a figure she had learned to know very well come from the other end of the house and go down the garden walk. Somehow it had become quite a usual accident that she should meet him and talk a little by the summer-house. Now she moved from the window, went quickly downstairs and out through the garden, until she found him. He was standing, as was his wont, looking out over the fields. He had scarcely time to hear her step and turn, she came so swiftly.

"Captain von Barheim," she began. He was so happy that she should openly seek him, that at first he noticed nothing; but in a moment he saw how white she was, how the dark shadows lay under her sweet, tired eyes.

"Mademoiselle, what is it? What has troubled you? Can I do anything for you?"

"You can do nothing but listen to me for a little," she answered; and folding her hands quite tightly, as if afraid to lose hold of herself, she looked at him and went on: "I wish to tell you that under the mistaken idea that I was aiding my poor country, I have done you a grievous wrong. I have taken your letters; I have destroyed them; I have read them." Here the blood rushed to her face, and left it again whiter than ever.

"I wish you to know it, Captain von Barheim, and I wish to beg your pardon." And she bowed her head like a culprit.

"Ah, you brave and generous girl!" he cried, looking down at the pretty crisp hair, and the white eyelids that hid her eyes from his gaze; and taking her hand, he kissed it with tender respect. She drew it away, but without anger; she only said, —

"I am neither generous nor brave. It was a mean and cowardly act;" and again she looked at him, all her impetuous spirit in her violet eyes.

"But how many far worse deeds are done in the name of patriotism!" said he. "And now you must listen to me, for I also have a confession to make. Last night I found a shoe, — a very small and pretty shoe. I thought it fair contraband of war, and meant to say nothing of it, but keep it. Now, I want you to tell me that I may have it. No, do not refuse until you hear me!" he went on quickly, for she shook her head. "This morning we have orders to march, and in an hour I shall be gone from this place, where I could have been, where I have been, so happy, — happy in seeing you every day. You will let me take the little shoe with me; and some day perhaps, some day when there is peace between our people, when the bitterness has passed away, may I not come again to you?" and the big fellow's voice failed him, and he was silent.

"Alas!" she cried, raising her streaming eyes and clasping her hands, "that day will never come!"

He spoke no word, but took her hand again and looked at her.

"Yes, you may keep it," she said.

He touched the top of her head with his lips, and released her, and she went away weeping. He made no attempt to follow her, but only stood and gazed until she was gone into the house.

She went to the window where she had watched them come, — these hated enemies. She hid herself no more, but sat there, very pale, watching the preparations for departure. At last he and the two young men mounted their horses in the courtyard and rode slowly out through the gate. She bowed courteously to the young lieutenants. Von Barheim came last, and never took his eyes from her face as he went. When he turned the corner of the road which would hide him from her view, he stretched out one hand toward her, and she answered with hers. Then the sound of horses' hoofs grew faint in the distance, and all was silent. The old life had come back, but never to be the same again.

Claire went to the garden terrace and sat down on

the low wall, looking out to those distant blue hills. Did their mystery hold any boon for her?

At déjeuner, Tante Artémise said, —

"Well, child of my heart, they have gone, as you know. They really made but little trouble, and the Captain left the politest of notes for me, thanking me in all their names for the courtesy shown to them here. Really, it is almost a pity that young man is a Prussian!"

And Claire said nothing.

"Do you suppose they ever met again?" said Muriel, a little wistfully.

"No, I don't think they ever did," said Bell.

"Why not, — with the world so small, and the war over?"

"Because, as a rule, people *don't* meet again. The world may be small, but it is wide enough for episodes and unfinished romances. Now, I should n't at all wonder if the French girl's brother came back after the siege of Paris and brought some brother officer with him, of a neighboring family, perhaps a good 'parti,' and all that. Then naturally a match would have been arranged in French fashion, and there! The matter is finished!"

"But for all that they may have met again," ventured Ralph.

"Yes, they may have," said Bell, "but let us hope, in that case, that they did not. Don't make a tragedy out of the little interlude!"

"As we can all have our conjectures," persisted Muriel, "I shall cling to mine. And I think, as a rule, that people *do* meet again!"

*Say, what abridgement have you for this evening?
What mask? what music? How shall we beguile
The lazy time, if not with some delight?*
     A MIDSUMMER NIGHT'S DREAM.

I am never merry when I hear sweet music.
    THE MERCHANT OF VENICE.

EVENING OF FIFTH DAY.

"It's an off-night to-night, is it not?" said Ralph,—"a 'relâche.' I wonder if the rest of you who have 'spoken your pieces' feel as relieved as I do! Just as I used to feel at school, on Exhibition days, when the fathers and mothers all came, and we had to get up one by one and recite something, or be examined in history or spelling. When my turn had come and gone, and I was not positively disgraced in the eyes of the world, and it was the next boy's turn, — oh, how good the apple tasted which I bit surreptitiously under cover of my desk! I believe you are the next boy, Margaret, are n't you, for to-morrow evening? But how comes it that you two are let off so easily, Mrs. Chauncey and Mr. Professor?"

"I am not so sure the Professor *is* let off," said Margaret. "I dare say he will have a Sunday story to tell us. We shall see."

"As for me," said Mrs. Chauncey, "you know I never meant especially to be here at all, so of course I brought no story. I have had a hundred dancing in my head in these last days, but none has written itself down. Besides, there are not enough days in the week."

"Alas!" and "Alas!" was echoed round the room.

"For myself," said Charlie Wyatt, "I have not the least idea what day it is, nor what any of the days have been,—except that they have been happy and golden, and that they will never be again!"

"What are we who have passed our examinations supposed to have instead of the surreptitious apple?" asked Bowdoin. "What are our prizes?"

"Suppose we give ourselves up to unlimited music to-night," suggested Ralph. "I can think of no better reward of merit. And, Margaret, your hoarseness seems to have quite disappeared; suppose you begin! Play to us first, and make us happy, and then you can sing and make us wretched if you choose."

Margaret went to the piano and played for half an hour, — Chopin, Schumann, Rubinstein. Her voice was a rich contralto, made of music in every tone, and she sang with a fine dramatic spirit. After a moment of searching in her memory she sang: —

"Oh, think not to win her,
    Luckless besieger!
  High on her battlements
    Sitteth she ever.

"Dead in the moat beneath
    Lie all thine arrows;
  They scarcely have frightened
    The two small sparrows

"That build 'neath the window,
    Whence listless, secure,
  She watcheth thine essay
    Hour by hour.

"But know that another
    Will come from afar,
  At the blast of whose trumpet
    Her castle's strong bar

"Shall fly from its socket,
    And drawbridge clang down,
As quick from her turret
    She hastens alone

"To hold but his stirrup,
    To kiss but his sword,
To call him her master,
    Her lover, her lord."

"Where did you get those words, Margaret? I never heard them before," said her sister.

"They were written by a friend of mine, and I set them to such music as you have heard." She ran over the keys for a little while, and sang again: —

"It was on this coast the ship went down,
    Here in the sight of land,
God's sky above, and the angels there
    Stretched never a helping hand.

"It was on this beacon rock she struck,
    When the long rough voyage was past;
The harbor light burned clear and bright,
    And home was reached at last.

"In the deep blue sea of thy tempting eyes,
  Close to thy heart of stone,
A soul was lost from Paradise,
  And a freighted life went down."

"I did not mean to sing anything sad to-night," said Margaret, "but I am afraid none of my songs are very gay. I see you have brought some music from the yacht, Mr. Wyatt. Do sing this one, won't you?" She held out a song in manuscript to Wyatt, who took the seat she had left, and sang: —

"The long gray island fades into the night,
  The misty sails glide out beyond the bar;
Trustful and grateful to the constant light
  Flashed from the lighthouse tower so high and far

"I, on the verge of this far vaster sea,
  Put out alone beneath these starless skies,
But turning, kneel and bless you; changeless still
  The light that never dims within your constant eyes."

As Wyatt finished, Erin, who had been lying quietly on the rug by the fire, suddenly began to howl so long and mournfully that he was very depressing, and it required a good deal of soothing on his mistress's part before he could be restored to his usual cheerfulness.

"And quite right he is," exclaimed Mr. Bowdoin, who had been out of the room for some time. "I never could understand why a pleasant evening should be turned into a vale of tears. I knew how it would be when Margaret began to sing, although at first she drew it mild. So while you have been amusing yourselves with being miserable, I have been preparing for you a salad, the like of which you never imagined. Come into the dining-room and cheer up!"

*Let us go hence, my songs, she will not hear,
Let us go hence together without fear;
Keep silence now, for singing time is over,
And over all old things, and all things dear;
She loves not you nor me as all we love her,
Yea, though we sang as angels in her ear,*
   She would not hear.

*Let us rise up and part; she will not know;
Let us go sea-ward as the great winds go,
Full of blown sand and foam; what help is here?
There is no help, for all these things are so,
And all the world is bitter as a tear,
And how these things are, though we strove to show,*
   She would not know.
                                    SWINBURNE.
   "*Et in Arcadiâ Ego.*"

SIXTH DAY.

"It is indeed a house divided against itself, to-day," said Mrs. Temple, as they were assembled around the breakfast-table. "Let me see if I have understood the programme. You have petitioned for the hammock and your book, Bell, and Mrs. Chauncey is coming over to help you to be idle; Tom is determined to leave no bluefish uncaught in the bay; four of us are to ride to the Barnstable Great Marshes; and Mr. Wyatt — what shall I say of him and his defection? I could not have believed it of you," she said, turning to him.

Antinous looked sore distressed. "Indeed, indeed," he stammered, "I never would have done so stupid a thing. I would get off now if I could. But I promised to sail in this regatta long ago, before I knew, before I — and my yacht is entered, and we must go in, unless I maim her or myself somehow, which I have a great mind to do. There never was such hard luck."

"Where is the regatta?" asked Muriel.

"The start is somewhere just outside of Mattapoisett Bay; I don't quite know the limits of the race. I have n't taken much interest in it lately. My skipper knows all about it. He thinks the 'Hope' is sure to win."

Muriel was standing in the porch, and the two walked slowly down the garden path.

"Perhaps she will win if you will wear her colors," he said, and stooped to pick a blue corn-flower, which the girl put in her white dress.

"I hope you will win the race, with all my heart," she said simply.

"I must go now," said Wyatt. "Will you let me see you alone this afternoon, Miss Carr-Wynstede? Before the sun goes down, not only the fate of the 'Hope' must be settled, but my own." And ere she could speak, he was gone.

It was a very long ride to those wonderful Great Marshes and back, and Mrs. Temple was surprised when Muriel told her, on their return, that she had promised Mr. Wyatt to walk to the headlands with him to see the sunset. Margaret was going to remonstrate; but the girl took her hands and kissed her on the forehead, and said, —

"Dear Mrs. Temple, I have promised. Will you trust me that I am meaning to do right, and let me go?"

"My child, I trust you wholly; go," Margaret said.

There is a picture by Sir Joshua Reynolds of a smiling landscape, and in the background a tomb, with the inscription,

ET IN ARCADIÂ EGO.

Death even in Arcadia! And sorrow there, and disappointed hopes, and broken hearts. For Pan is dead, and the happy, careless Fauns and Dryads are gone, and mortals have dared to enter in, taking their burdens with them, which even there cannot be laid down, — even in Arcadia!

"*I hear a voice you cannot hear.*"

> *. . . for they, at least,*
> *Have dreamed that human hearts might blend*
> *In one, and were through faith released*
> *From isolation.*
>   MATTHEW ARNOLD.

> *And love will last as pure and whole,*
> *As when he loved her here in Time,*
> *And at the spiritual prime,*
> *Rewaken with the dawning soul.*
>   TENNYSON, *In Memoriam.*

> *Oh days and hours, your work is this:*
> *To hold me from my proper place*
> *A little while from his embrace*
> *For fuller gain of after bliss.*
>   IBID.

EVENING OF SIXTH DAY.

"MURIEL tells me that we shall not see Mr. Wyatt again," said Margaret that evening. "He was obliged to leave very suddenly, and had to catch a favorable wind. He sent many farewell messages, and wanted us to know that the 'Hope' had lost the race."

There were all sorts of exclamations of regret and surprise, and Mrs. Temple trusted devoutly that Muriel's pale face and trembling fingers passed unnoticed, as she sat at the farther end of the room, her head bent over her embroidery. To prevent troubling questions, Margaret said, "And now, if you are ready, I will tell you my story. I shall call it

THE VOICE.

MOST of you knew Eleanor Gray, so I need not ask if you remember her. She was a creature not to be forgotten. And you know too that she was my most dear and intimate friend; yet it was but a short time before her death that she told me the secret of her life. There was always about her, even to me, and in spite of our real intimacy, a vague sense of something mysterious; of unsounded depths, of a life lived apart, into which I did not enter, to which I held no key. One day, here at Fair Harbor, sitting with me on the very headland from which Muriel saw the sun go down this afternoon, she told me her story. While she lived, it was sacred; but I can tell it now without disloyalty, and I will. I do not ask for your belief or disbelief. I can give it to you very nearly in her own words, for I wrote it down almost immediately after hearing it from her lips, I was so anxious to remember it exactly; and I read it over last night to refresh my memory.

It will explain much that seemed singular in Eleanor's character and life; and if you wonder at the facts I shall relate, at least you will acknowledge their consistency with what you knew of her. When I went to Europe years ago, I left Eleanor Gray a lovely young girl; she was several years younger than I, you know. I came home, to find her a beautiful woman. I had always been very fond of her, but now she attracted me wonderfully, and drew me to her with a different and compelling charm, — not alone on account of her great beauty, her grace, her exquisite sweetness and womanliness, but from something, I could not tell what, which put her quite apart from other women, and inspired in me a sort of reverent feeling. Tennyson's "In Memoriam" was constantly in my mind when I looked at her, and her life seemed to furnish a sort of context to that most spiritual of love-poems. And yet I had not known of her having had any heart-grief, and no one could tell me of her having lost any near friend while I was away. There were moments when she seemed not to be in this world at all. "Her eyes were homes of silent prayer." The dreamy, yearning look that came into them when she sat quietly, her beautiful hands folded before her, seemed to penetrate the mysteries of unseen places; and sometimes a strange, sudden look of rapture lighted them, such as we may have seen on the faces of the dying.

And yet Eleanor's life was by no means that of a dreamer. We know how full of work it was, how full of gracious employment, of loving help and sympathy and comfort. She was the light and embellishment of the brilliant assembly, as she was the angel of mercy in the homes of the poor and suffering. Her time and her self were at the service of any who needed them. The world was brighter and better because she lived in it.

> "For she had learned the creed of creeds,
> The loveliness of perfect deeds."

She was never in what we call "high spirits," and yet I think she was quite the happiest person I have ever known. To be sure, it is only repeating myself to say this, for have I not said that her life was lived for others? Her own beautiful nature had taught her the secret which people go through life without learning; longing, struggling to find Happiness; looking for it in all the unlikeliest places, — from mountain-tops of success and renown; wearily seeking the philosopher's stone or the alchemist's elixir; asking it of youth, of pleasure, of gold. She only looked straight before her and around her, and saw that

> "all worldly joys go less
> To the one joy of doing kindnesses."

To men she was irresistibly fascinating. They fell in love with her in season and out of season, as if fore-ordained and predestinate thereto. They simply could not help themselves, and never blamed her for it; so she kept them always as friends, after she had declined them as lovers.

I was often made the confidante of these unlucky loves; and the only consolation I could offer was the quite true, if insufficient one, that if she did not care for them, at least she cared for no one else. And sometimes I went so far as to remonstrate with her upon her indifference, when some one unusually attractive presented himself as a suitor only to be dismissed like the rest. Then she would look very sorry and very grave; and once she put her hands in mine and said, "Ah, my dearest Margaret, some day you shall know!"

Just before we came here together, at the time I referred to, a friend of mine came to see me and told me that he had asked Eleanor Gray to marry him, and had been rejected. As he talked of her, his handsome face full of emotion, he showed such manliness, such a depth of devotion, such a passion of tenderness, that I found myself wondering that any woman could say him nay.

"I love her with my whole heart," he said; "I shall love her till I die. I am not worthy of her; what man is? I wonder I was ever so bold as to confess my love to her. And yet, I am glad she knows it. And for myself, I am very proud of it. Do you know," he asked, "if she has ever cared for any one? No! do not answer. I have no right to ask. But she told me she should never marry, and I believe her. I believe she has no heart to give. She seems to me like a vestal virgin whose heart is vowed to Heaven, or like a woman who has had one absorbing passion in her life, of which the object is absent, perhaps what we call dead, yet ever living, ever present, to her."

I had so often felt exactly like this about Eleanor, that I started to find my thought echoed.

"I can never cease to care for her," he repeated, "never fail to be her loyal friend and true knight; and such service and devotion as I may give her, will make my life richer than would the love of any woman on earth."

One does not find such chivalry every day, and this man was a special friend and favorite of mine; and altogether I could not help feeling vexed with Eleanor, though he would not let me say so.

A little while after this interview we two came to Fair Harbor together. Eleanor was very fond of this region, and we often came here, or somewhere in the neighborhood, for a week or so, in the spring or autumn. On the afternoon of which I have spoken, — a beautiful afternoon in June, — we had been sitting yonder at the head of the bay, watching the ships go by in the glow of the sunset; neither of us had spoken for some time, when I said by a sudden impulse, —

"Eleanor, Hugh Endicott told me that he had met with the common fate. Forgive me, dear, but if you only could have cared for him! He is so clever, so handsome, such a noble fellow. He seems to me the fine flower of our best civilization, — a sign to the rest of what New England can produce; his career has been so brilliant and honorable; he is interested and active in all good things. What do you desire more or better, Eleanor? How can you help caring for him? Truly, I do not understand."

While I spoke eagerly, hurriedly, Eleanor's face grew pale and flushed by turns. She began to speak, stopped, hesitated, and then raising her beautiful eyes to mine with that ineffable look in them, she said, —

"Margaret, I want to tell you now, *why!* Will you listen?

"Four years ago, just before you came from Europe, the year of my twenty-first birthday, indeed on the evening of that very day, I went to a dinner-party given by Mrs. B. I remember, as if it were yesterday, every detail of that evening. I remember the dress I wore. It was all white, and I had white roses at my belt and in my hair. All the time I was dressing I had a strange sense of something *impending*, something very solemn and very unusual. I had never felt anything like it before; it made me feel very happy, but awe-struck. I went through my toilet as if I were in a dream. When I came downstairs, I saw my mother look at me. Then she came to me, and without saying a word, kissed me on the brow; and my brother, who was going with me, said, 'Why, Eleanor, you look — you look somehow like a bride whose lover is going off to the war!' How often I thought of his words afterwards, and of their unconscious prophecy!

"When we arrived, and were shown into Mrs. B's drawing-room, the guests were all assembled, and very soon dinner was announced. Mrs. B. came toward me with a gentleman whom I had not seen, as portières had been between us, and said, 'Eleanor, I want to present Captain Fortescue, of the English army;' and she told him to take me in to dinner. Our eyes met; and oh, Margaret, that first look! It seemed to me as if my whole being were centred and fulfilled in it; as if I had been waiting for that moment all my life long. I took his arm, and we went in to dinner. It was a brilliant, gay dinner. I believe there were fourteen guests besides ourselves, but I cannot remember, I do not think I ever quite knew, who the others were. I was on the left of my host, and on his right was the lady for whom the dinner was given, so he talked principally with her. He must have observed my absorption, but I doubt if the rest did especially; at any rate, I did not care. From the moment I sat down, my eyes and ears, my heart and soul, were *given to him.* It was an absolute, unconditional surrender of myself. We talked of many things, — of books, of music, of American and English politics, of some of the deeper things of life; of each other; and as we talked I felt with startling conviction that we sympathized absolutely, radically, on every subject. It was wonderful. At last I asked him how long he had been in Boston. 'Not yet one whole day,' he replied. 'I came this afternoon, and ' — he hesitated; I looked up at him; all color had left his face, and his voice faltered — 'and I must go away to-morrow !' I forced myself to speak, but only to repeat his words: 'You must go to-morrow !' 'Yes,' he said. 'I had a cable message just before I came here this evening. My regiment is ordered to Zulu-land, and I must start directly to join it. I sail from here to-morrow !' And then, before I could answer, something happened ! A Voice, clear and distinct as mine speaking to you now, but which had in it no earthly sound, it was so pure and silvery, said close at my ear, 'Tell him that you love him ! You may never see him again in this world ! Oh, let him know it now !'"

Eleanor paused for a moment, and bowed her head. I put my arms round her without a word. Presently she raised her head. Her eyes were shining with an unearthly, holy light. She seemed to be listening again to some voice I could not hear. Then she went on : —

"I hardly know what happened for a moment after that. I think I must have been almost unconscious,— out of myself, as we say. When I next heard a voice speak, it was his own, but in a hushed, low tone, as if to himself, —'Oh, my God, if I dared !' I am sure my agitation must soon have been perceived by the rest of the company, but in a very short time my hostess made a move, and the ladies left the dining-room. Captain Fortescue excused himself from returning with the gentlemen, and said he must go to his rooms to pack his trunk, as he was to sail the next morning. He walked beside me to the door of the drawing-room without a word; but as he bade me good-by he took my hand in his and said, 'Will you give me one of your white roses?' I gave it to him, and he said, 'I shall write to you, may I? And we shall meet again !'

"After that I don't at all remember what passed, nor how I got home. I believe some of the women rallied me on my 'conquest,' as they called it, of the 'handsome English officer,' but I did not heed, and scarcely heard them. I only knew that I had bidden him good-by; and I kept saying to myself all that night : —

'But in my spirit will I dwell,
   And dream my dream, and hold it true,
   For though my lips may breathe adieu,
I cannot think the thing farewell.'

"Three weeks from that evening," Eleanor said, after another pause, "I was walking home alone, across the Common. It was a mellow afternoon in November. The sun had just gone down, leaving a rich crimson-and-gold afterglow in the western sky. The church towers and spires beyond were lighted up, and showed through the almost leafless trees in front of me like beacon-lights pointing to heaven. There was no one near; I could hear no footstep but my own, and no sound but the dropping of the autumn leaves, and the rustle of them as I walked. Suddenly, close at my ear, came the silvery tones of *the Voice*, the same which spoke to me that evening, in the supreme hour of my life. It said, 'Wait! It is only for a little while. If the Dawn tarry, wait thou for the Dawn.'

"Nearly a month passed away, and then I received through Mrs. B., the lady at whose house I had dined, and addressed to her care, a thick letter from Natal. I had never seen his handwriting, but I knew it was not he who had addressed that letter. I broke the envelope, and two letters were inside. The first I read was from a brother officer, and was very brief. It told me that his friend Captain Lionel Fortescue had gone into battle directly after his arrival with his regiment at Natal, and had been struck down while leading a charge against the Zulus at Bushman's River Pass. He lived only a few hours, long enough to write the enclosed lines, and to charge his friend with his dying breath to see that they were sent. He also asked that a withered white rose, which was found where he indicated, should be buried with him.

"*His* letter I can repeat to you word for word," Eleanor said, "for I say it over to myself every day. He wrote: 'My darling, when I bade you good-by that night, I said we should meet again; and now I know more certainly even than I knew it then, that we shall. That night we were betrothed to one another forever. We needed no word of declaration or assent; and yet, I wish I had told you then that I loved you. I wish I had obeyed the Voice that spoke to me; for as surely as it is sure that my soul and body will be parted ere another day dawn, did I hear a Voice which was not of this earth say to me as we sat together, "Tell her now that you love her! You may never meet again in this world. Oh, tell her, tell her now!" And I only said to myself, "Oh, my God, if I dared!" I know now that it would have been no daring; that I might have spoken and told you the truth. But it is only for a little while that I leave you, my own, my bride, my love! God is very good, and it will not be for long. So I wait till you come to me, beloved, there where there will be no seas between, and no partings.' It ended here. In the other letter his brother officer said that he had left him for a moment while he was writing, and came back to find him lying still on his camp-bed, asleep, he thought; but when he went close and spoke to him he found that he was dead. So," said Eleanor quietly, "I wait, dear friend; it can only be for a little while, and God is very good. I am content to wait."

Soon after she told me what I have faithfully related to you, her sister's little boy, of whom she was devotedly fond, was attacked by scarlet fever. Eleanor insisted upon nursing him, and he died in her arms. She took the disease herself, you remember, and died after a few days. I did not see her again till after her death, and then I begged to be allowed to go into the room where she lay. She never looked more beautiful in life. There were white roses on her breast and in her hands, and on her face, whiter than the roses, was the look of rapture and of sight.

I stooped down and whispered, "This kiss is for your bridal day, my darling!"

Muriel stood at her window that night, and the waning moon looked mournfully in at her. Deep in her own soul was a great new joy, the thought of which raised a tumult of happy heart-beats; yet to-night she almost reproached herself for being happy, as Wyatt's sad, pleading face came up before her, and the tones of his voice full of passionate despair.

Outside, the moon's pale rays shone down upon the gray water; all else was darkness. The watch-light was gone; the vigil was over. The rote of the waves as they broke on the bar sounded to Muriel, with their sad monotonous refrain, like the sob of farewell words, and the sighing night-wind bore to her ears the eternal murmur of "the unrecognizing sea."

To pray together, in whatever tongue or ritual, is the most tender brotherhood of hope and sympathy that men can contract in this life.
MADAME DE STAËL.

It is those who understand what a church is, who are the least likely to rest in it, or in anything short of Him to whom it leads.
DORA GREENWELL.

O heart of mine, keep patience; looking forth
As from the mount of vision, I behold
Pure, just, and free, the church of Christ on earth,
The martyr's dream, the golden age foretold.
WHITTIER.

The American Church is the great total body of Christianity in America, in many divisions, under many names, broken, discordant, disjointed, often quarrelsome and disgracefully jealous, part of part, yet as a whole bearing perpetual testimony to the people of America, of the authority and love of God, of the redemption of Christ, and of the sacred possibilities of man. . . .

We look on, and far, far away we see the Nation-Church, the land all full of Christ, a true part of the World-Church, issuing into glorious life and swallowing up our small ecclesiasticisms, as the sun grandly climbing up the heavens swallows up the scattered rays which he sent out at his rising.
PHILLIPS BROOKS.

SEVENTH DAY.

As they were driving home from church this Sunday morning Margaret said, "Look at those cabbage-fields, — those happy cabbage-fields! Why don't poets and painters make more of them? With their many beautiful shades of purple, blue, and green, like the sea along the Riviera, and their look of plenteous and absolute content, they are a delight to my eyes. If there were not an unreasoning prejudice against them as an unæsthetic article of food, if they could be called by another name, they would be sung and painted, I have no doubt. In that matter of names Shakespeare made his one foolish remark."

"I have often wished to write the epic of the cabbage-field," said the Professor; "and as to pumpkins, just look at that glorious pile of them against the gray shingled farm-house yonder, — the farm-house with the lean-to roof, and the well-sweep, and the festoons of dried apples hanging from the roof, and the herbs drying in the sun. What a picture!"

"Stop for a moment at Captain Nye's door," said Margaret. "I want to ask Mrs. Nye at what hour she expects us to tea this evening."

Mrs. Nye had but just got home from meeting herself, and stood at the door in a shining black silk dress, and Leghorn bonnet trimmed with dove-colored satin ribbon.

"We will have supper at seven to-night, if that suits you all," said she. "Father and I are so pleased that you're coming. I ain't seen father so happy about anything for ever so long."

"It is to be the best evening of the week for us, dear Mrs. Nye," said Margaret. "I wanted my friends to have the pleasantest for the last."

As they drove away from the door, the old Captain came round from the barn, where he had been putting up his horse.

"Father," said Mrs. Nye, "what do you think about it?"

"Think about what? I was wondering why the brindle had n't given as much milk as common for two days past."

"Father," said Mrs. Nye solemnly, laying her hand on his arm, "do you remember what I said to you about Mis' Temple and that Professor when they rode by on horseback the other afternoon?"

"Bless my soul, Martha, how you womenfolks do go on! You know you would have it our Dick was going to marry Lawyer Willet's daughter the second time you ever saw them together."

"Well, and was I right? Did our Dick marry Lawyer Willet's daughter, or did he not?"

"Yes, he did, if it comes to that," acknowledged the Captain. "But that don't prove folks are always thinking o' marrying; and I never see the man yet I thought good enough for Mis' Temple."

"Well, I hope you church-going people enjoyed your church and your sermon," said Bowdoin, who had not been.

"I enjoyed both greatly," said Muriel. "What a dear old man the clergyman is, and what a comforting, helpful sermon he gave us! Our rector at home is such a dreadful pessimist, it always takes one a week to recover from the depression of the Sunday before."

"Yes," said Margaret, "I always think of those lines of Matthew Arnold's when I hear such a sermon as that, and when I look at Mr. Hall's life. Do you remember, —

> 'And yet it seemeth not to me
> That the high gods love tragedy,
> For Saadi sat in the sun,
> And thanks was his contrition:
> For haircloth and for bloody whips
> Had active hands and smiling lips;
> And yet his runes he nightly read,
> And to his folk his message sped.
> Sunshine in his heart transferred,
> Lighted each transparent word;
> And well could honoring Persia learn
> What Saadi wished to say.'

It is really an excellent description of Mr. Hall. He does incalculable good in his parish by just living and being what he is."

"It is a pity more of his calling were not like

him," remarked Tom Bowdoin. "Generally speaking, I should apply to them and to many of their congregations what somebody or other said, — 'The paucity of Christians is remarkable, considering the number of them.' And as to going to church, I have no objection to any one's going if they like. For myself, I prefer — " and he drew a long puff at his cigar.

"Yes, I know; I have heard a good deal about that," said Margaret.

"About what?" asked Tom. "I had n't said anything."

"No; but I know what you were going to say, — that God can be worshipped as truly in the fields and woods as in a church; that the groves were God's first temples; about looking from Nature up to Nature's God, — I have heard it all, often, and I don't deny that there is something in it. A reverent soul lifts itself to its Maker anywhere, everywhere, and never more fervently perhaps than when in the midst of the beauty which comes straight from His hand for our joy and thanksgiving. But lively emotions of gratitude for God's goodness, springing up constantly in a man's breast, argue a religious spirit; and a religious spirit is apt to express itself by direct acts of worship. Such acts are naturally performed in the modes and places which mankind has for ages regarded as most fitting; and so the majority of the civilized world has agreed to gather together on certain days, at stated times, to express in divers fashion their love and gratitude, and to ask for help and forgiveness."

"Then you think church-going the absolute test of piety and religious feeling," said Bowdoin.

"By no means; no, indeed," replied Margaret warmly. "Some of the most truly spiritual people I have ever known have never entered a church since they began to think for themselves. I have even known very good people who seemed to feel a sort of revolt and disgust for all kinds of external religious manifestation. I had one dear friend, an eminently religious man, who tried hard to cure me of going to church, and thought it unworthy a woman of sense. He used to shudder with contemptuous horror when he saw the black-robed High Church fathers go by my window in their 'pitiful petticoats,' as he called them. But such persons are rare exceptions, and dangerous exceptions besides."

"Why dangerous?" asked Bowdoin; and the Professor looked up eagerly, to see what Margaret was going to answer.

"I wish some one else would speak," said she, blushing. "Why do I seem to be preaching a sermon myself? I am sure I never meant to."

"Please answer my question," urged Bowdoin, — "why dangerous?"

"Because they set a bad example, I cannot help thinking. Because this very talk about worshipping God in His works is initiated and encouraged (sincerely, I have no doubt) by such persons. And just because they are good men, whose lives are above reproach, they are pointed at (by the illogical) as proofs of the good effects of non-churchgoing; and unfortunate instances of men who *do* go to church, and yet who are dissolute or dishonorable, who lie or cheat or embezzle, are brought forward (also by the illogical) as evidence of the little good, if not of the absolute harm, of religious forms and observances. That is why it seems to me that men or women who stay habitually away from church, no matter *how* excellent and moral their lives may be, are setting bad examples, and in so far are dangerous in their day and generation."

"What do you think about it, Miss Carr-Wynstede?" asked Ralph.

"I quite agree with Mrs. Temple. And I have noticed one thing at home. The people who don't go to church, and talk about it being quite as well to say one's prayers in the woods and fields, don't seem to me to go into the country on Sundays with that view, though I may do them injustice. I dare say one's frame of mind *may* be as religious in strolling about one's grounds, or sailing in one's yacht, or driving about the country, as in going to a service in church, only it don't look so, you know."

"But one shouldn't mind the look of the thing, should one, so long as the thing itself is no harm," said Bowdoin; "and whose business is it, after all?"

"If every one of us lived on an island of his own," the Professor said, "that would do very well. But as we none of us can escape the responsibility that comes from our all being members of one big family, the lives we lead and the examples we set do come to be the business of all the rest, down to the minutest particular, it seems to me."

"If we had an established church in America, as you have in England, Miss Carr-Wynstede," said Tom Bowdoin, "there would be some satisfaction in belonging to it. But here, where in every little village there are half a dozen different sects, all quarrelling and disputing among themselves and with their neighbors, there seems to be no rest for one's soul. If I had the power, I would decree that henceforth in all America there should be, literally, one faith and one baptism, and an American church; and all outside of it should be under the ban, and looked upon as dissenters and heretics. Then I would be a Churchman myself."

"I have heard Tom talk like this before," said his wife, "but I cannot really think he is in earnest. I certainly do not agree with him in the least."

"Ralph," said Margaret, "do you remember when we were at Woodstable one autumn, years ago, when Mrs. Stuart was with us, and would n't go to 'meeting,' but rode or drove or sailed on Sundays? She was a Churchwoman, and did not consider the little Methodist place of worship church at all. I always thought she made a grievous mistake, for she either hurt the feelings of the townspeople by seeming to despise their humble meeting-house, or else gave them to suppose that she had no respect for Sunday and no religion at all herself. I wonder if she ever considered the bad example she set to the young people in that village, or how many Sabbath-breakers she is responsible for to-day?"

"As far as I am concerned," said Mrs. Chauncey, "I like to go to church, and always do when I can. When Paul and I were in Europe, we always used to go to the English churches on the Continent, when there were any. The only thing I objected to was praying so often for the Queen and the royal

A Week away from Time. 321

family, — begging your pardon, my dear Miss Carr-Wynstede! I was always quite willing to do it once; but when it came to five or six times in one morning service (and the service so long any way), it was too much, and I just did n't do it, and tried to think of something else. If once is enough for our President, it is enough, or ought to be, for the Queen. I did n't at all blame a little boy who said to his mother, 'What a very wicked family it must be, mamma, to need so much praying for!'"

Muriel laughed at this, but said her laugh meant no disloyalty; and then she said very seriously, "I was in Boston only two Sundays, but two Sundays meant going to a certain church four times; and I wondered, as I looked round at the vast congregation which filled every seat and every corner, if they truly appreciated the privilege it was to live in a city where their souls could be fed and their lives guided by that inspired preaching and teaching. I wonder still. Sometimes what one has, what is so freely given, comes to be looked upon as a matter of course."

"The same question has often occurred to my mind," said Professor Kirkland. "It seems to me that the responsibility in this case is as solemn as the privilege is great; and that if the sheep hear the voice without heeding it, — if they 'look up and are not fed,' because of their own insensibility and hardness of heart, they will be in more woful condition than if they had never come near the fold."

Joy is the vital air of the soul. Health is the first of all liberties, and Happiness gives us the energy which is the basis of health. To make any one happy, then, is strictly to augment his store of being, to double the intensity of his life, to reveal him to himself, to ennoble and transfigure him. Happiness does away with ugliness, and even makes the beauty of beauty. In Paradise, then, every one will be beautiful. For, as the righteous soul is naturally beautiful, and as happiness beautifies all that it penetrates or even touches, ugliness will have no place in the universe, and will disappear with grief, sin, and death.

AMIEL, Journal Intime.

Happiness is cumulative, as misery is. Happiness has no limits, as heaven has neither bottom nor bounds, and because happiness is nothing but the conquest of God through Love.

IBID.

EVENING OF SEVENTH DAY.

THE afternoon had been passed in various ways by the friends who knew that it was the last. Muriel and Ralph had wandered off, over the hills and far away, and came home just in time to get ready for Mrs. Nye's tea-party. Margaret and her brother-in-law had driven to Wood's Holl to make some visits, and she told Bell to make the most of the hammock, to be covered with plenty of wraps, as the air was cool, and to let the Professor stay with her under the lindens; "for," said she, kissing her sister and blushing rosy red, "he has a secret to tell you, which is mine too, and which I want him to tell you himself."

Mrs. Chauncey said she should go to her hotel and write letters and take a nap, and would join them at the farm-house at seven o'clock. "I never did take tea in a farm-house," she said, "but I should think it would be delightful. It reminds me exactly of the Cotter's Saturday Night, only that this is Sunday."

We are apt to say that a table "groans" when it is laden with good things; but it would seem an inappropriate phrase, as if the table were unsympathetic and ungracious, and bore its burden grudgingly. Mrs. Nye's table did not groan; it fairly laughed and clapped its leaves, and overflowed with gladness at its own good cheer. There never was such a tea-time, — oysters of the sweetest and rarest, in the shell and escaloped; cold roast chicken and ham and tongue; and a smoking hot pasty, out of whose flaky depths came quail and partridges and all manner of riches; and hot biscuits, white and light as snow just fallen; and waffles and griddle (or *girdle*[1]) cakes; and such honey from her own bees; and such preserves and plum-cake; and, as the feast's perfect and consummate crown, the Quahog cakes.

"That any one should dream that he knows what Quahog cakes can be until he has eaten

[1] *Scotticé.*

these, or having eaten these, that he should ever try to have them made at home, seems to me the acme of human folly and conceit," exclaimed Margaret; and they all cried, " Hear, hear!" And Mrs. Nye's purple cap-ribbons trembled with pleasure, and her whole benevolent, bountiful person shone with content.

"Dear Mis' Temple," she said, "I felt real bad at first when you took the White House and settled there, 'cause it seemed somehow as if we was going to lose you! But I declare for 't, I 'm just as glad now as I can be, for we have n't lost you a bit; and as I said to father, it 's as good as Thanksgiving, any day, to have you and your friends sit down at our board to-night."

After supper Mrs. Nye showed the way into the parlor, or "sitting-room." This was a solemn occasion, and worthy of the room, which was seldom used except at times of peculiar import, such as weddings, sewing-bees, or funerals. A fire had been lighted there some hours before the guests arrived, so that there was none of the musty, uninhabited flavor of rooms which are not used as "living rooms." But it did have an aromatic, Oriental, delicious odor of its own, and it was full of handsome and curious things which the old captain had brought home long ago from his voyages in foreign lands. There was a Russian samovar, and two big Chinese bowls, one filled with "pot-pourri" made of rose-leaves and lavender and rosemary and white lilies and all sorts of sweet-smelling dead petals which never die, and the other full of fresh marigolds and gladioli and mignonette and pansies and sweet peas and many-colored asters and bright autumn vines. The mantel-shelf was decked with rare and beautiful shells, and on the floor were some old Turkey and Persian rugs. Several pieces of old oak furniture, with shining brass trimmings and claw feet, looked as if they had been in their places since Colonial days. An inlaid cabinet from Japan stood in one corner, filled with cups and saucers, plates and tea-services of old Lowestoffe and Chelsea and Delft ware. There were handsome brass andirons and fire-irons, and a fender of fine workmanship, which would have excited the covetous desires of any connoisseur.

"How have you been able to keep these beautiful things from the hand of the spoiler?" asked Mrs. Bowdoin. "I have friends in Boston, who I truly believe, if they knew of their existence, would break and enter, and get them from you by fair means or foul."

Mrs. Nye laughed good-humoredly. "Why, you wouldn't believe the things ladies have done," said she. "They have come from miles around, — from Wood's Holl and Falmouth and Cotuit; yes, and from Mattapoisett and Marion and Monument. Some comes and makes a pretence of asking their way, and saying they're tired, and may they come in and have a glass of water, and so works the conversation round. And they coax and wheedle and bribe, and some of them have got real right-down mad when I wouldn't sell 'em at any price, and said things — well, it made me feel bad to think a lady should say 'em. But it's never been any use their getting mad, and it never will be. Father began to bring me these knick-knackeries before we was married, — when he was courtin' me, — and kept right on as long as he went to sea (except some of that chany and furniture that are heirlooms); and do you suppose I am going to let 'em go for money? No, not till father and I are starving, which, please Heaven, we hope that time will never come. No, they 'll go to our son Dick that 's married and lives out West, and 's got a likely wife and children; except one or two, which I will say, Mis' Temple, I 've seen you admire, and we 've testamented 'em away to you."

"Indeed, it will be a sad day for me when I see one of them in any room but this, dear Mrs. Nye," said Margaret affectionately.

The Captain, who had on his best Sunday black wig and sharpest-pointed shirt-collar, around which was a black satin stock which made him a little stiff-necked, now came toward Margaret, and said a few words in a low voice, looking at the Professor as he spoke.

"Very well," said Margaret. "The fact is, Mr. Kirkland, I told the Captain, when we first came this evening, that you had something you had promised to read to us if we had stayed at home to-night, and which I had induced you to bring with you."

"I am afraid it is too serious for so festive an occasion," said Kirkland.

"Oh, do let us hear it, Professor," urged the Captain. "Why should n't we have something serious? We are serious folks, I hope, all of us, in one sense; and if the Professor will do us the honor to read what he has brought, I am sure we shall never forget his goodness. I speak for mother, I know," said the old man, "and I guess I speak for all this company."

"Then here goes," said the Professor, "I can't resist such kind words as yours, Captain; and if the others find my essay on Happiness more than they can bear, I shall not be in the least hurt if they leave in the middle of it."

HAPPINESS.

Not long ago I listened to the discussion of a very interesting question, — a question that may be said to have had a place in the speculation of human beings of all times; no less a question, in short, than how to be happy, or, in other words, what quality, or attribute, would lead to the greatest attainment of happiness. It was very interesting to listen to the modes by which one or another thought that happiness was to be achieved, if achieved at all. Some, indeed, felt as if we might as well begin by relinquishing the expectation of happiness at first, not attempting to cheat ourselves into a hope which could never be realized; or again, with Carlyle, that happiness was not even to be desired, but that we should substitute *blessedness* for happiness, and count ourselves the better off for the change. In fact, as at the beginning of all discussions, one must clear the ground by finding first what people mean by the words they use; for the same words are used to mean a thousand different things, according to the temper or the complexion of him who uses them; according to his sentiment or condition; according to the lines of thought or action at a given time; or even according to the conventional standard of a certain period. There are cheap and superficial ways of using noble words, there are partial and personal ways; and in the confusion of ideas which results from all this, no wonder that we hear so many half-truths spoken; no wonder that some say there is no such thing as happiness, and others that if there be such a thing it is unattainable by mortals. Yet, at the same time, whether there be happiness or not, we must remark the deep and pathetic witness borne to the craving for it in the human breast, in the very frequency and variety of the definitions given. For all the way from Socrates to Schopenhauer, many wise men and every thinking man have set themselves to defining in some shape or other this condition of the soul which we call happiness.

Now, I cannot help thinking that here, as well as in regard to all our most serious convictions, we want to ask ourselves what we mean when we ourselves use this word; what deep idea we associate with it, what spring of action is furnished to us. Is happiness to be regarded as rightly attainable, or is it to be set on one side as unworthy the interest or aim of thoughtful people?

At the outset of such a discussion one is often met by those who beg the question; asking how it is possible for a sympathetic soul to be happy in the midst of a world's misery; or if suffering, and not joy, is not the only true discipline; or if happiness does not tend to enervation and indolence? As I make these running suggestions of the current phrases which are used in this connection, I am sure you will all recognize them, and add to them fuller and further varieties of the same questionings. I speak of them because they show how large a temptation there is to accept half-truths, or to dwell upon the superficial aspect of truth, and how often this superficiality leads to a fatal misunderstanding of first principles; the danger of a little knowledge, not because it is small, but because in our ignorance or our stupidity we call it large. And chiefly do we find, in considering questions of this import, how seldom we allow for the relations of things. We seem to live out our own lives, not in one large airy sphere of thought and action, but in little separate worlds of existence, where in each the small circumference hems us in, and keeps our spirits and our reasons bound round, hopelessly withheld from contact with the rest. We are like children who possess a fund of unrelated matter. We have a knowledge, in short, of the details of living, but not of the philosophy of life.

But let us begin at the beginning: 1. Is there such a thing as happiness? 2. What is it? 3. How does it come? Our first question gets its answer from the lips of human experience. We know that there is such a thing as happiness because we have felt it. After the manner of Descartes' famous argument for existence, — *Cogito, ergo sum* ("I think, therefore I am"), we may argue from the emotion to the fact, for all have known the note of joy. It matters not at this point what were the causes, what the sources, or what the permanence of happiness; it is only to bear testimony to the fact that at some beautiful moment, remote or near, we could call ourselves *happy*. So far it is not difficult to get an answer to our question. But though all may know that there is such a thing as happiness, and be able to vouch for its existence, it is by no means so simple a matter to say *what* it is; and here indeed we find, as I said before, an endless variety of definition. To get at its meaning we need to analyze this emotion, this rapture, if we may; to discover what happens in us by virtue of which we become aware of a feeling which is like no other feeling, — in short, to know what we mean when we say we are happy. Perhaps we get a clew in the point upon which I take it for granted that all would agree, — the nature of happiness. Every one would admit that the sensation is not contrary to our nature, but in harmony with it; it is a verification, not a contradiction of our personality; something that we call *native*. When one is happy, one does not seem to go forth into a strange country, but to enter into one's own land. When one is happy, one feels no consciousness of restraint or limitation; in short, when one is happy, what is it but to feel free? I think in the last analysis this is happiness, — *a sense of freedom*. But this freedom depends upon what? And so we are brought to the third division of our question; for the way in which the happiness or freedom comes is through the exercise of power for a given object. I think if we take the end of this thread in one hand and slowly unwind it, we shall find it leads us into the heart of a great and beneficent mystery which we have not begun to understand. We shall find, first of all, that it is by fulfilling the laws of one's spiritual nature that one perceives the joy of living to be a glorious reality. And as these laws are many and various, so there are many manifestations; and yet all are good, and all noble, if only they spring from a noble use of power. Perhaps the first and most important thing to take note of in this conception of happiness is that it becomes not a *result* so much as a *state of being;* that is, it is not a possession that we clasp, which we long to get, or which we fear we shall lose, — not of this meaning or purport is joy, — but we are in it, are one with it, and so, finding ourselves, cannot be rid of a certain glorious condition. It involves the same analogy as that by which the truth makes men free; by the exercise of intelligent desire they achieve the knowledge of the truth, and in so achieving they are made free. Now, what is the assertion that we are virtually making, if we ascribe this place to happiness? We are acknowledging that each human being comes into the world endowed with certain potencies or capacities for good, and that these capa-

Happiness. 337

cities developed to their results produce the complete individual, that human result which we believe to have been in the thought of the Creator regarding each one of us; and in becoming that thing which we are meant to be, we find joy. It will easily be seen that this way of looking at life, at the same time that it admits happiness to all, by no means excludes pain. On the contrary, the powers which we exercise the oftenest, involve suffering, discipline, sacrifice, grief. These well-worn but never out-worn modes of experience form the channels in which we labor to gain our ends, to produce our results; but we claim that so long as one is free to use some or all of the gifts God has given him, there is a central place in the soul where one may be said to be *happy*.

Perhaps the first and most general illustration of this comes in the doing of healthy work. Those who have never *thought* about this see the result without understanding the reason for it. One hears it said, in familiar phrase, that people are "happier" for being employed; but few ever dream of the essential freedom which willing labor bestows, by virtue of which those who toil earn a sweetness of reward all unknown to the idler and the slave. Of course, the more intelligent the labor, or the more noble or enduring the results, the greater will be the satisfaction of doing it; but even in the lowest forms there comes the pleasure which is the germ of more complete delight, in the mere iterated doing of simple and homely acts which involve a successful use of power for a given purpose.

There is so much to say here. The question of labor is one full of problems, and so, full of interest; we meet them on every side. There are those who contend that man labors only under the compulsion of acquiring the necessities of life, — because he must; while on the other hand those who claim the distinguishing prominence which marks the human from the brute world to be the "law of progressive desire," insist upon a spring of action that makes labor a normal condition of human existence. But apart from all these theories, it is getting more at the root of the matter to say simply that man is a moral being, committed by his nature to the fulfilment of moral purposes; and that for him accordingly all forms of labor are beautiful and sacred because they belong to the development of moral order. So, whether work be done by the miner in his shaft or the student at his book, it all has the stamp of nobility, being essential to the world's need.

Again, judged by our test happiness reaches a level of great fulness in the service which we can render to those who are in need; for here it often happens that all our powers are best brought into exercise. We may labor with our hands for their bodies, we may labor with our spirits for their souls, and in the blessed stress of sympathy find manifested to our hearts yet deeper depths of the joy which comes with each act of patience and of faith.

Nor let it be forgotten that the splendors which wait upon the service of humanity are the direct gift of Christianity; Christ having gathered the separate sparks of human fellowship which were lit in the breasts of all who would serve their fellow-men, — of Moses and David, of Epictetus and Socrates, — and laid them on one altar of brotherhood as a quenchless flame which shall not go out day nor night forever. This brotherhood may suffer at men's hands on one side, so long as selfishness and injustice still have sway, or, on the other side, it may be perverted nobly but falsely into a system of religion where man usurps the place of his Maker, as in the Positivism of our day; but broad and strong between these misdoings and misconceivings runs the stream of Christian fellowship, with infinite interchange of loving service, with infinite sources of happiness. Before Christ came, the principle of fraternity existed as a rudiment; with Him it became a ministry and a vocation, and in its ceaseless development it has included the world, filling the web of life with countless offices of mutual confidence and support.

Especially does it behoove us to remember this with gratitude here in America, — America, which is so far the largest and, thank Heaven, so far the most successful experiment ever tried on the basis of fraternity. That none shall be left in ignorance, that no limit shall be set to free development, that every man's conscience shall be held sacred, — this is the service to which we are committed in our country. Is not this a noble freedom; and, worthily fulfilled, would it not lead to peace and joy?

So much for the test which may be applied in our life with others, and in the multitudinous relations which that life involves. But we shall find that the individual life also presents sources of happiness, no matter under what press of circumstance or weight of misfortune it may be led.

One of the wisest and sweetest of philosophers once wrote these words: "For if good in its essence be in those things which depend upon ourselves, then there is no place for jealousy or envy; and you will not wish to be a general nor a prince nor a councillor, but to be free, and to this there is but one way, — disdain of the things which depend not upon ourselves."

This has long seemed to me to be a great lesson in

the art of living, for it brings us to the immediate consideration of the great fact that along with the life of service and companionship runs the life of independence and of solitude; while the exercise of power for and in others is largely achieved by its exercise for and in our own souls also. Indeed, we may say that no one can largely help others who has not brought into control his own nature. Otherwise his sympathy is no better than that of a little child, which may solace but cannot support the suffering spirit. He who would bring another into the way of peace needs to have set foot therein; for those who invite with most persuasive or most compelling force are they who say not *go*, but *come*.

So the gift of happiness awaits the exercise of those powers of the soul which have to do with the most intimate personal life, — the acts of faith, the acts of patience, the acts of loyal love, things done for the strengthening and renewal of the soul's forces; or, again, the solitary resisting of temptation, the abnegation of self, the loneliness of the darkness and the cloud, if only therein it may draw nearer to God. Let it never be forgotten that it is our glorious privilege to find joy in pain, to suffer and yet be strong, to take the world as it is and to find in it the assurance of the heaven that shall be. Discouragement, it sometimes seems to me, is a loss of memory; it can only come when we forget why and what we are.

So far we have spoken only of the freedom which we gain by acting upon our inner impulses, the spring of action which comes to us in a certain sense from within. But what shall we say of that great province of refreshment which comes to us in the form of gracious gifts, — the gift of beauty, the gift of love? These bestow happiness also in accordance with the same principles. All about us lies a world full of mysterious suggestion, of infinite charm and variety, yet the charm rests not in the thing itself. Nature on one side, and art on the other, — *open gates* through which the imagination may go free and find delight.

"Thou hast set my feet in a large room," David said of it. And who does not know what the perception of Beauty may mean to the cabined spirit? how a blade of grass or a patch of sunlight can unloose to a soul the splendors of the spiritual universe, can free it from the blackness and the baldness of prosaic existence in making it feel the power of its perceptions, the glory of its intimations?

Who cannot find joy in a world where each soul may, after its own measure, claim the heritage of which Wordsworth tells in his invocation to Toussaint?

"thou hast great allies,
Thy friends are exultations, agonies,
And love, and man's unconquerable mind."

The gift of Beauty and the gift of Love. If we end with Love, it is because we must also begin with it. From the mother's embrace, which gives a first direction to the young soul, all the way through, perhaps, to some consummate human love, its meaning is but one and the same, — a more perfect freedom. It takes us a lifetime to understand this in its fulness. While we are children, obedience is the type of freedom, and after we have left the narrower walks of childhood, and have become men and women, it may be that we shall call it *consecration;* but, by whatever name, it is freedom still, and the freedom that comes through love is the best of all, because Love not only *allows* but *invites* the soul to enter upon its own, or even runs before with willing feet to show us what we are free to be.

I have left no room, nor could I venture to speak of what may be discovered when in the fulness of a mutual love one reaches to the very heights of freedom. This is an open secret, a truth greater than any proof of it can be. As such I leave it.

But the happiness which all may share, this also is real; this is inseparable from right living. Some things we may have; this we must have Sick, sorry, and suffering we may be,—all these we undoubtedly shall be, so long as life lasts; but happy we *must* be whenever we do one loyal deed or follow one star of duty. Happy, because we fulfil our divine nature therein; happy, because we serve others; but, far deeper still, happy because we are unconsciously made one with the Divine Will.

After Mrs. Nye's guests had said good-night and good-by (for they were going to leave Fair Harbor the next morning), and Mrs. Chauncey had assured her hosts that she had never had such a delightful evening in all her life, "especially those heavenly cohort cakes," she said, the good old couple stood together under the stars, and watched the retreating forms till they could no longer be seen.

"Well, father, what do you think now?" said Mrs. Nye.

"I think you were right, mother, as you mostly are, and I think that Professor is one of the noblest men God ever made; and I think he is good enough for Mis' Temple, God bless her! I can't say more 'n that, can I?"

"Wasn't it beautiful to hear him read his discourse in that fine, manly voice; and did you notice Mis' Temple's face, and see how starry-like her eyes were, and how proud and happy she looked? I guess she's come as near finding out the secret of happiness as folks often does; and if ever a woman deserved it, she's the one."

"Amen to that!" said the Captain.

"But that ain't all," pursued his wife. "I don't suppose you noticed anything between Mr. Ralph and that handsome young English lady, did you?"

"Oh, come, mother, I can't take in so much all at one time! You do beat all! I've got enough to think over now; you can't be pairin' off everybody. I dare say you'll be makin' a match between Jim Canaan and the French Mamzelle, they bein' about the only single ones left to speculate on."

"I might make a crazier speculation than that," answered Mrs. Nye, shaking her head mysteriously. "This has been a terrible interestin' week for the folks at the White House, you'd just better believe me!"

"I do believe you always, mother," said the Captain affectionately; "and there's one thing I know, — that they can't none of 'em choose wiser than I did, nor live happier than you've made me live, not if they try ever so!"

Mrs. Nye gave her husband a kiss for all answer, and they went up the little garden walk, back into their peaceful home.

As the others were walking slowly by the path through the fields to the White House, the Professor said, "Who can remember those lines from Matthew Arnold's 'Empedocles on Ætna'? Charicles' song, is it not? It begins

> 'Where the moon-silvered inlets
> Send far their light voice.'

It is running in my head to-night, but I can get no farther."

"They are favorite lines of mine," said Margaret. "I think I know them. I believe I was thinking of them just now myself: —

> 'Where the moon-silvered inlets
> Send far their light voice,
> Up the still vale of Thisbe
> Oh speed and rejoice!

'On the sward at the cliff-top
    Lie strewn the white flocks;
On the cliff-side the pigeons
    Roost deep in the rocks.

'What forms are these coming
    So white through the gloom?
What garments out-glistening
    The gold-flowered broom?

'What sweet-breathing presence
    Out-perfumes the thyme?
What voices enrapture
    The night's balmy prime?

''T is Apollo comes leading
    His choir the Nine;
The leader is fairest,
    But all are divine.

'Whose praise do they mention?
    Of what is it told?
What will be forever?
    What was from of old?

'First hymn they the Father
    Of all things; and then,
The rest of immortals,
    The action of men;

> "The day in its hotness,
> The strife with the palm;
> The night in her silence,
> The stars in their calm.'"

Nobody went to bed very much that night. Muriel was closeted for some time with Mrs. Temple; the two sisters had a long talk together, and finally Margaret and Ralph, far into the night. As Ralph left her room, she said,—

"Then you go to see Muriel's parents to-morrow? Bell is very anxious to know if you have kept 'Lady Barberina' sufficiently in mind. She goes all lengths in admiration of Muriel, but 'Lady Barberina' troubles her."

"Yes, I am going to-morrow," said Ralph, "in spite of 'Lady Barberina.' I cannot believe it, even now, Margaret. Great Heaven! It is inscrutable! That she can possibly care for me! And yet, she has said it!"

The brother and sister stood hand in hand for a moment without speaking. Then he took her in his arms and whispered, "My dearest, I would not give you up to any other man in the world! But you and Philip are worthy one of the other. God bless you, as He will forever!"

The last morning had come, the last farewells had been spoken, and Margaret was left alone at Fair Harbor.

"It has been a wonderful week," Bell had said, "and it is a wonderful Gulf Stream! I believe in it! I salute it! It is a marvel-worker, a magician, a fateful stream!"

Margaret stood in the sunshine, her faithful dog by her side.

"Erin," she said, "you remember my dream of the springtime! It is autumn now, but my dream has come true!"

THE END.